How to Help Your Dyslexic and Dyspraxic Child

How to Help Your Dyslexic and Dyspraxic Child

A practical guide for parents

Sally McKeown

white
LADDER

First edition published in Great Britain in 2011 by White Ladder Press
This reprint first published in Great Britain in 2022 by White Ladder
An imprint of Hodder & Stoughton
An Hachette UK company

1

A CIP catalogue record for this title is available from the British Library

Paperback ISBN 978 1 90541 096 5

Typeset by IDSUK (DataConnection) Ltd
Printed and bound in Great Britain by Clays Ltd, Elcograf S.p.A.

Hodder & Stoughton policy is to use papers that are natural, renewable
and recyclable products and made from wood grown in sustainable
forests. The logging and manufacturing processes are expected to
conform to the environmental regulations of the country of origin.

Hodder & Stoughton Ltd
Carmelite House
50 Victoria Embankment
London EC4Y 0DZ

www.hodder.co.uk

Contents

About the author

In a former life Sally McKeown was a teacher, working in schools and further education. For five years Sally ran a large basic skills unit working with young people who had dyslexia, dyspraxia and related conditions. She found that many of the conventional ways of teaching did not work for them. In later years she worked in the field of literacy and special needs for government agencies and also earned her living as a journalist.

In the course of Sally's working life she has interviewed many parents and children. This book contains some of their stories, which will inspire you and help you to help your child.

Acknowledgements

Many people contributed their stories, their time and their skills to bring this book to publication. I would like to thank Mick Archer, Beth Bishop, Louise Boulden, Sarah Cooper, Emma Haley, Clare Hargreaves, Jeff Hughes, Diane James, Joe McKeown, Amanda McLeod, Jane Mitchell, Barbara Morrison, Tina Morrison, Keith Murphy, George Nestor Allen, Tine Norling, Christine Toal, Rachel Womack and staff at Earlsdon Library. Particular thanks are due to Ben, Chloe, Jake, Matt, Rupert, Simon and Helen and former students of the Ben Unit in Coventry. Thanks also go to educational psychologist Dr Mark Turner for casting his expert eye over the book.

Foreword by Tom Pellereau, winner of *The Apprentice* 2011

Inventor Tom Pellereau secured a £250,000 business investment from Lord Sugar on The Apprentice *in July 2011. Here he talks about the impact dyslexia has had on his life.*

Dyslexia is tough but it has always been a massive positive for me. Everyone has unique skills; dyslexia means you become good at adapting and finding ways of solving problems. Your brain offers hundreds of different ways to solve the problem, which stands you in good stead.

My dyslexia has been a big influence in my life and success as an inventor. I seem to see things differently to others and create many solutions that may not have been thought of before. I find visualising simple. When I have an idea, I can picture it in my brain and spin it around. My experience of having dyslexia has also made me very tenacious and hard working. At school it seemed I had to work twice as hard just to keep up. This is something that has always stayed with me and helped hugely as I've got older. As things haven't always come easily, I know to never give up, as there is always another way.

When I was at school I struggled with English and languages, I remember a new English teacher brought in a class rule that any spelling mistake found in an essay had to be written out correctly 20 times. In my first essay I made over 100 mistakes, which made for a lot of extra homework! These experiences also made me comfortable with failure. This is crucial, as failure is a vital step on the route to success. From a young age I knew I was very bad at certain things, but I had a clear sense of the things I was good at too. In my case that meant I was always going to do science, engineering and design.

Many young people with dyslexia or dyspraxia get disheartened. I know that I was one of the lucky ones. My first school recognised my dyslexia early and provided extra lessons. I also had great support from my parents who would always say 'well done' and 'keep going'. I used to make things and take them apart when I was a child and my Mum and Granddad encouraged me in this. I knew they valued what I could do instead of always focusing on the things I was bad at. This helped me to become confident about my own abilities and I worked harder at the areas where I could succeed.

Computers with a spell checker were a life-saver for me. I was so lucky that computers came out when I was starting to write essays. The very first computer my Granddad gave me was [one of Lord Sugar's] Amstrad 1512s. With hard work, focus, a lot of help from others and computers I gained three As at A level and a First Class Honours degree with a master's in Mechanical Engineering with Innovation and Design.

I won *The Apprentice* against a lot of competition from highly talented people who did not have dyslexia or similar difficulties. I believe my dyslexia helped me to develop products, find different solutions to tasks, deal with losing tasks and work with others.

With the ever increasing improving technologies that help spelling, reading, grammar, memory and other things many hurdles are being removed. In tomorrow's world creativity and attitude will be the key to success. These are areas that dyslexics can excel at and I believe there has never been a better time to be dyslexic.

I really believe that there is no reason why people with dyslexia and dyspraxia cannot achieve. We may have to work harder and find our own way, but we will get there in the end! Anything is possible really, just remember there is always a way.

Introduction

People pick up a book like this for many reasons. Maybe you have just found out your child has dyslexia or dyspraxia and want to find out as much as possible so you can reassure your child and help him to make satisfactory progress at school. Perhaps you have a date for an assessment by an educational psychologist and want to find out what is likely to happen. Maybe you just suspect that your child has a problem and want to be better informed, especially if you are going to talk to your doctor or to a teacher or find other sources of professional help.

There's a lot of information about dyspraxia and dyslexia available to parents. Just look at the books on Amazon or in your local library. You have probably read a few of them yourself and might have checked out the websites of some of the specialist charities. However, lots of the information comes from a medical or educational perspective, looking at symptoms, causes and interventions. But what about the practical side? How do you help your child cope with the frustrations? How do dyspraxia and dyslexia affect family life? And what can you do about it?

How to Help Your Dyslexic and Dyspraxic Child covers everything you need to know: from the emotional impact on the family through to sources of help available to you. Above all, it has practical ideas for things you and your child can try. It features the experiences of six children and their parents and one adult with dyslexia. In the first chapter of this book, we'll introduce them and their stories, and you'll also hear from them throughout the book as they share their experiences and give advice to families going through similar things.

Perhaps, like Ben, your child has been identified as having problems very early on and you are working with nursery or school to make things better. But maybe, like Jake, your child has been assessed much later. His mum, Tina, had been trying to cope with Jake's problems on her own for a long time and they received the diagnosis only when he was in his final year at primary school. Some children are diagnosed even later. They might have left the school system and started at a college of further education or university. This means that they will have had many years of education struggling with problems when they could have been receiving help. If you suspect your child has undiagnosed dyslexia or dyspraxia, do speak up. Sometimes a busy teacher will spot only those with the most obvious indications of a specific learning difficulty, so a child who is bright but underachieving may slip through the net. This book will show you different ways of approaching professionals.

Perhaps your child is like Rupert, who has both dyslexia and dyspraxia. This means that he has problems not only with words and symbols (dyslexia) but also with the messages from brain to body (dyspraxia), so he may also find tasks involving fine motor skills or organising himself a challenge. We have covered both dyslexia and dyspraxia in this book because there are many overlaps between the two conditions. They are part of a group of related conditions called specific learning difficulties. Both are neurological so they are permanent conditions that affect the way in which the brain works and processes information.

Many parents ask what the future holds for children with specific learning difficulties so we also include the story of Helen, who grew up with dyslexia and is now a mother herself. She has been through many of the things your child may be facing and has developed her own way of coping with day-to-day aspects of adult life – from managing money to learning to drive. There is no cure for dyslexia or dyspraxia. They are lifelong conditions but thankfully many children find ways to cope with the difficulties they cause. This book brings together tips and advice from our families and also draws on some of the concerns and comments from the excellent web forums where parents share experiences and help one another.

It is so easy to see the downside of dyslexia and dyspraxia, especially on days when the frustration levels are high – why does your seven-year-old daughter always look so untidy and how does she get cereal in her hair every morning? Why can't she recall the spellings she knew perfectly last night? Why is your son in a permanent fog? He has lost his house keys for the second time in a month, just after you had changed the locks, of course, and you have no idea why he didn't turn up for his interview. Yes, the parents in this book have been there and done that. But amid all these frustrations remember that dyspraxia and dyslexia can also be the catalyst for great talents. One of my favourite comments is from a contributor called misspiggy, who has written on the beingdyslexic.co.uk forum.

> 66 *Being able to decipher writing is really a tiny skill that has taken over the educational system by a freak of fate. A lot of people who do well at school would be eaten by sabre tooth tigers very quickly indeed if they lived in the Stone Age, whereas dyslexics would be inventing wheels and things because of their ability to link ideas together creatively.* 99
> **misspiggy**[1]

Author's note

The Dyspraxia Foundation says: 'Dyspraxia is thought to affect up to 10% of the population and up to two per cent severely. Males are four times more likely to be affected than females'; while Dyslexia Action figures show that 'three times as many boys as girls receive additional teaching because of their dyslexia'.[2] In view of these figures, we have used 'he' throughout the book unless we are specifically referring to a female.

What does it feel like to have dyslexia or dyspraxia?

Frustration, rage, anxiety, protectiveness: it is a curious emotional cocktail for parents when they have a child who has dyslexia or dyspraxia. The children are bright, intelligent and creative – they can paint wonderful pictures, make music or be the world's expert at a computer game – but there are things that they just can't do. There seems to be a gulf between their innate ability and their performance. Perhaps they struggle with basics such as knowing their times tables or tying up shoelaces, or their difficulties might be more momentous, such as not being able to read at all or walk downstairs, or being prone to sensory overload and becoming so overwhelmed by noise and lights that they cannot cross a road safely.

Take a case featured in the *Evening Standard*. The article 'The dyslexic boy failed by the system' describes a 10-year-old boy in

London, 'David', who has a reading age of a child aged four years and four months. His schooling has been a disaster and, according to educational psychologists' reports seen by the *Standard*, he has progressed 'just one month in five years'. His mother, Margaret, is fighting to get the council to fund him to attend a special school for severely dyslexic children. Margaret said: 'It would cost the council £37,000 a year to put him in a special school, but they have dragged their feet and only this month got him statemented. It is a tragedy because my son is now so far behind his peers that he will never catch up.'

She is now taking the council to a tribunal and feels that her son's dyslexia has taken its toll on all the family. 'The whole ordeal has been hugely stressful and has affected my marriage,' she said. 'I hardly sleep, my brain won't switch off, I'm on the phone to solicitors and writing to experts every day, trying to fight for my son's future, for his right to have a stake in society. If I don't fight for him, who will? He's not stupid and he has a fantastic memory, so there's stuff to work with, though his self-esteem will have to be rebuilt.'[3]

However, for every child like David, there are many children with dyslexia who make progress when they work hard with a specialist teacher in a mainstream school. Ben, who you will meet in a moment, is a case in point. But equally there are times when you might face obstacles and feel frustrated and this book will give you the tools to talk to the school and do the best for your child.

A word of warning here: a book like this cannot help you to diagnose your child. Only an expert can do that, but you need to learn more about dyslexia, dyspraxia and other related conditions so you can see where your child's problems might lie. Dyslexia and dyspraxia are part of a family of specific learning difficulties which all centre on how the brain processes information. Different types of specific learning difficulty affect different functions.

- Dyslexia: problems with acquisition and processing of language and linking sound with letters.

- Dyscalculia: a difficulty with numbers and mathematics.
- Dysgraphia: a difficulty with writing – both handwriting and composing coherent sentences. It may appear in children who read quite well.
- Developmental co-ordination disorder (DCD): problems with fine and gross motor skills. It is what used to be called 'clumsy child syndrome'.
- Dyspraxia: the brain has problems organising movement so children may have problems with motor skills, with language or with organising their thoughts.
- Attention deficit disorder or attention deficit hyperactivity disorder (ADD or ADHD): concentration difficulties with heightened activity levels and impulsiveness.
- Asperger's Syndrome and autism: issues with communication, imagination and social interaction. It is sometimes characterised by rigid, repetitive behaviours.
- Tourette's Syndrome: tics – involuntary and uncontrollable sounds and movements.

In this book we focus on dyspraxia and dyslexia as these are the most commonly identified conditions. Some children are very clearly in one category but others may have more than one specific learning difficulty. As mentioned earlier, Rupert, one of the children featured in this book, has dyslexia and dyspraxia. Simon has behavioural difficulties as well as dyslexia and is currently being assessed for ADHD.

As a parent you need to be aware that these conditions represent a pattern of difficulties and you cannot pigeonhole children. Matt has many of the classic symptoms of dyspraxia but he can catch a ball. If a child has dyspraxia, some parents will realise something is wrong very early on. Perhaps your child is very late in walking, falls over more than the average child or just cannot go up and down steps. Dyslexia is less obvious in the early years and usually comes to light when a child starts reading and writing and, in the school's words, 'fails to make satisfactory progress'.

Only an expert can find the right diagnosis for your child's particular pattern of difficulties, but, as you read this book, do look at the information for both dyspraxia and dyslexia because there is a crossover between the two conditions. Do not be afraid to mention both when you are talking to teachers and other professionals.

The good side of dyspraxia and dyslexia

You are probably living with a very special, creative person who has an unusual take on the world. Dyslexia, dyspraxia and creative ability seem to go hand in hand. Just look at the Extraordinary People website, at www.xtraordinarypeople.com. Daniel Radcliffe (Harry Potter) has dyspraxia, as does Marco Pierre White, and so did the poet Coleridge. There is a galaxy of stars in all fields who have dyslexia. It's not just the artistic types, such as actors Eddie Izzard, Ben Elton, Dustin Hoffman and Keira Knightley or musicians such as Noel Gallagher, Robbie Williams or John Lennon, or artists such as Andy Warhol. There are many chefs, including Jamie Oliver and Rick Stein, not to mention some of the big names in science: Newton, Faraday, Edison, Bell and Einstein. Then there are sporting heroes: Jackie Stewart, Dennis Bergkamp, Steve Redgrave, 'Magic' Johnson and Muhammad Ali. There are also lots of successful writers: Agatha Christie, Lynda La Plante, Hans Christian Andersen, W. B. Yeats and F. Scott Fitzgerald obviously didn't find that poor spelling held them back.

Business brains

According to Professor Julie Logan, entrepreneurs in the UK are twice as likely to be dyslexic as the general population. She found that dyslexic people display better skills in oral communication and problem solving. They are also likely to be better at managing staff, having developed delegation skills in order to cope with their conditions. 'People with dyslexia start their own businesses so they can control the environment around them, do what they're good at and bring in other people to compensate for what they're not good at,' she says.[4] This may explain why so many famous names from the business world are reputed to have dyslexia or dyspraxia. There's Mr Microsoft, Bill Gates, and Mr Apple, Steve Jobs, not to mention Ms Body Shop, Anita Roddick, and F. W. Woolworth. Tom Pellereau's creative and inventive mind also helped him to become the 2011 *Apprentice* winner, in a new version of the show which looked for an entrepreneur with a great business idea, rather than simply an employee.

In fact, there is a school of thought that sees dyslexia as a positive advantage. Sir Richard Branson, who has both dyslexia and dyspraxia, claims: 'Being dyslexic can actually help in the outside world. I see some things clearer than other people do because I have to simplify things to help me and that has helped others.'

But let's move away from the rich and famous to meet some of the young people featured in this book and see how they cope.

Matt's story

Matt is 13 and has dyspraxia. He lives with his mum, brother and sisters in Gloucestershire. He stays with his dad at weekends. He was in a state primary school but it did not meet his needs and so he moved to a private school. He is now in a private Catholic secondary school and has shown an aptitude for maths.

His mum Clare recognised that Matt had problems from an early age but he was not diagnosed until he was at school.

> 66 Matt was always different from the word go. He reached development milestones later than his brother and sisters and had some coordination problems. He walked a bit later than his brother and sisters and found it hard to ride a bicycle. He somehow could not get the concept of turning the pedals to make the bicycle move. He would do a bit and then stop. 99
> **Matt's mum Clare**

Jake's story

Jake is an only child. He is 17 and lives with his mum Tina in Warwickshire. Like Matt, he has dyspraxia. He is currently studying for his A levels in maths, chemistry, physics and photography at a state school and hoping to go on to university.

> 66 *I was initially frustrated with Jake, feeling that if he just tried a bit harder he could do things better. Because he came across as an articulate and intelligent child, I couldn't understand why he was having such a problem with 'simple' things and I would become impatient with him, which upset him, and subsequently upset me. You can't help making comparisons with other children, particularly when they are young and passing those important milestones. I'm sure we all have great expectations, especially with our first ones!* 99
> *Jake's mum Tina*

Rupert's story

Rupert is 12. He lives with his parents and an older brother and sister in Gloucestershire. He has both dyslexia and dyspraxia. He started school in the private sector, which was not a positive experience, so he moved to a state primary school where he has flourished.

> 66 *The school could not understand why he could write some long words very accurately but could not write a word such as 'was'. They blamed him and said he was not trying. We had already had our oldest child assessed so I arranged to get an educational psychologist involved. He produced a report showing that Rupert had characteristics of both dyslexia and dyspraxia. He made a number of recommendations but after a couple of months the school had not*

implemented these so we looked around for a different school. We were fed up with him being labelled as lazy and he was suffering from the teasing and bullying from other children. 🙧
Rupert's mum Emma

Chloe's story

Chloe is 16 and has dyslexia. She lives with her parents and an older brother, Nathan, in Sheffield. She is taking her GCSEs and is planning to go to college to do a BTEC course. She had problems with reading, writing and spelling. Years of phonics and all those 'look, cover, write, check' spelling drills did not have any impact. She was a very angry child at one stage and was in trouble for bullying other children at school. Her mum read up about different approaches and has given Chloe intensive home support. Chloe wants to make a fresh start at college and has no intention of letting them know that she has a statement for dyslexia.

🙧 *Chloe was a happy toddler. She loved singing and dancing and was a real little performer. She loved playgroup and nursery so we had no worries about her starting school, especially as her older brother was already there. But she soon fell behind. She developed a 'thing' about reading and the more we tried to coax her, the more tearful she became, but if we stopped, the other children in her class would get further ahead and the more ground we would have to make up. It was terrible.* 🙧
Chloe's dad Will

Simon's story

Simon is 15 and lives with his mum and younger sister Molly in west London. In their early years the children were brought up to be bilingual (English and French) but since their dad moved out they just speak English at home. School has not been a happy experience for Simon.

> 66 *Simon hates school, he hates having dyslexia and he hates us. When he was excluded from secondary school I felt quite desperate. He had been given a laptop by the school because his handwriting was completely illegible but he did not receive any extra attention or support. His class teacher said that he was a gifted child who was just not trying hard enough. In fact he was angry and isolated. Here was a child who was trying to break through the wall between him and the school and he could not do it. He has been excluded several times at school, the last time for behaving dangerously during a chemistry lesson and the time before that was for destroying a laptop the school had supplied as part of a package of support for his dyslexia.* 99
> **Simon's mum Sofia**

Ben's story

> 66 *Ben was always a busy boy at home, on the go the whole time, but at school they said he was withdrawn. His teacher was really worried because he would not make eye contact with adults and tried to fade into the background all the time. He was not yet five years old, he had developed eczema and he was so tense he could not smile. We were devastated when the teacher told us all this. We did not realise it had got so bad.* 99
> **Ben's mum Sarah**

Ben is 11. He lives with his mum and dad and older brother in Pembrokeshire. He had tinted glasses at the age of six but he was still lagging behind. Sarah tells what happened next.

> 66 *I was working full time at a special school and, with worrying about Ben, I was getting worn out. My dad came across the Dore programme on the internet. I was doubtful when he told me because it seemed like a lot of money and I was worried about how to pay for it. My dad wrote a cheque there and then, so we had to*

do it! Ben had never watched a TV programme with us: he would watch for two or three minutes and then lose interest and go and kick a ball about. On Christmas Day, when he was a bare three months into the programme, we finally watched a whole film as a family. Sadly my dad did not live to see the results. 🔊
Ben's mum Sarah

Helen's story

Helen is an adult now with a 14-year-old daughter of her own. Helen has dyslexia which did not have a particular impact on her schooling but soured her relationship with her mother.

🔊 *She was a worrier and I knew from a very early age that I was a 'Problem' and a 'Disappointment'. My sister Maddy sailed through stuff and I always trailed along in her wake. We did not get on. I don't think there was any competition between us because I knew I would lose any contest so I never tried. Looking back, I don't think teachers worried about me nearly as much as my mum did. They thought I was just not a very bright kid. My mum was the one who took me for a private assessment. It just resulted in more homework, more specialist phonic tuition and more hassle. My education really took off when I left home.* 🔊
Helen

Families react in different ways when they find that a child is not progressing in the way that they expect. Some take it in their stride; others, perhaps like Helen's mother, feel that it reflects badly on them. Some want to 'cure' their child while others will deny there is a problem or see it as the school's responsibility. As well as the burden of day-to-day worries, many parents worry about their child's future. Maryanne Wolf is the author of *Proust and the Squid: The Story and Science of the Reading Brain* (Icon Books, 2008), but she is also the mother of a boy with dyslexia. In an article in the *Guardian* she wrote the following.

> ❝ *I am an educator and neuroscientist, who studies how the brain learns to read and what happens when a young brain can't learn to read easily, as in the childhood learning challenge, developmental dyslexia. Yet, despite this knowledge, I was unprepared to realise that my first son, Ben, was dyslexic. He was five years old when I put all the pieces together, and I wept as soundlessly and deeply as every other parent. I wept not because of his dyslexia, which I understood very well, but because I knew the long, difficult road Ben faced in an educational system ill-prepared then to meet his needs.* ❞
> *Maryanne Wolf*[5]

Do these ring a bell?

So what have our parents noticed? There are insights that will ring bells with many of you reading this book:

- 'I have learned that some of the filters that most of us have are just not there. He responds strongly to stimuli and is exceptionally aware of what is going on around him.'
- 'She is good at distractions and avoiding things she does not like. I hate the fact that she is so hard to pin down.'
- 'He responds well to routines and rules and that may be why he finds maths and science so much easier than subjects which require him to deal with ideas and nuances.'
- 'I have never known a child to be so disorganised. I could scream most of the time but he can be very funny too so I don't stay cross for long.'
- 'He has always found studying tiring. It requires heavy concentration. Learning vocabulary and spelling was hard – after 10 minutes he would be yawning.'
- 'He is socially inept and it drives me mad sometimes. He comes over as being rude or offhand and he doesn't mean it. At least, I don't think he does.'
- 'I really worried about him because he was excluded from all the things the other boys were doing.'

- 'People think you are a bad parent and that you should be controlling the child. They don't understand his frustrations.'

In the course of the book you will hear more from these children and their parents. These are people who have been through what you and your family are experiencing and can give you ideas about how to cope and make life easier. You will also meet a few experts who work with families and can help to ease the problems. But, for now, Tina has the final word.

> 66 Once I had a firmer understanding of why he couldn't do the things other children found easy, I felt terrible for my impatience and I became frustrated with other people, particularly the school for overlooking the positives and focusing on the negatives. I was (and still am to a certain extent) very protective of him. He was very vulnerable and I felt he was too easily dismissed as lazy and his confidence was very low. I was quite angry with his primary school as they just wouldn't listen to me and totally ignored Jake's difficulties. Even with an official assessment they still failed him as far as I can see. We handle things differently these days though; we've got our own strategies for dealing with everyday life and thankfully Jake is chilled and comfortable with himself. Things might take a bit longer but we get there in the end. Patience and a sense of humour are the two most important things we've learned on our journey so far! 99
> *Jake's mum Tina*

About dyspraxia and dyslexia

How many people have dyspraxia and dyslexia?

According to Dyslexia Action, between four and five per cent of the population have dyslexia: 'It is estimated that there are about 375,000 pupils in the UK with dyslexia and a total of some 2 million people who are severely affected.'

The Dyspraxia Foundation states that dyspraxia affects 'up to 10% of the population and up to two per cent severely. Males are four times more likely to be affected than females.'

First reactions

When you first suspect that your child has dyspraxia or dyslexia you probably find yourself scouring the library shelves and the web looking for information to confirm or allay your suspicions.

Here you will run into your first major stumbling block: dyspraxia and dyslexia are hard to diagnose and there are links with a lot of other specific learning disabilities, such as attention deficit disorder, some forms of autism or a communication difficulty. Children do not necessarily conform to the descriptions you may read in books, for example you might find children with dyslexia who read well.

> 66 *I thought all children with dyspraxia were clumsy, but Matt isn't. He had poor fine motor skills so he found it hard to cope with laces, buttons and ties but he was not noticeably clumsy. His father and brother are very keen on games and had played ball with him almost from birth, but while he is quite good at sport, he has problems recalling the rules for different games, especially rugby.* 99
> **Clare**

This book cannot offer a conclusive diagnosis for your child, but what we can do is show you the range of characteristics found in children who have been assessed for dyslexia and dyspraxia. You will find there is an overlap between different conditions and some children will have characteristics of more than one specific learning difficulty. Certainly, once you have found out more about the conditions, you will be in a better position to talk to a paediatrician, GP, teachers or a special educational needs coordinator (SENCO).

Self-esteem

Whatever your child has – dyslexia, dyspraxia or a blend of specific learning difficulties – one of the key factors is self-esteem. When children are marked out as being different, when they fall behind, it is not just the parents who worry. It is important that children do not see themselves as failures. They will need a lot of reassurance and you need to be on the lookout for opportunities to praise their efforts and achievements. Later in this chapter you will find information about left brain/right brain dominance. This may help you to understand why your child behaves the way he does, and, equally importantly, may help children to realise that they are different and can be just as successful as other children. In fact they may well have increased creativity and a problem-solving approach that will stand them in good stead. You will find more ideas about how to boost your child's confidence in Chapter 11, 'Dealing with daily frustrations and boosting self-esteem'.

Recognising dyspraxia

The Dyspraxia Foundation says: 'Dyspraxia is generally recognised to be an impairment or immaturity of the organisation of movement. Associated with this may be problems of language, perception and thought.'[6]

Children with dyspraxia are sometimes identified when they reach developmental milestones later than expected. These might include sucking, rolling over or sitting up. The Dyspraxia Foundation has a page called 'The symptoms' on its website (www.dyspraxiafoundation.org.uk). The section on pre-school children lists many of the symptoms that are most characteristic of this condition.

Dyspraxia checklist

Children with dyspraxia may demonstrate some of these types of behaviour:

- very high levels of motor activity, including feet swinging and tapping when seated, hand clapping or twisting, and inability to stay still
- high levels of excitability, with a loud or shrill voice
- may be easily distressed and prone to temper tantrums
- may constantly bump into objects and fall over
- hands flapping when running
- difficulty pedalling a tricycle or similar toy
- lack of any sense of danger (for example, jumping from heights)

- continued messy eating (they may prefer to eat with their fingers) and frequently spilling drinks
- avoidance of constructional toys, such as jigsaws or building blocks
- poor fine motor skills, such as difficulty in holding a pencil or using scissors, and their drawings may appear immature
- lack of imaginative play, for example they may show little interest in dressing up or in playing appropriately in a home corner or Wendy house
- limited creative play
- isolation within the peer group – children may be rejected by their peers and prefer adult company
- laterality (left- or right-handedness) still not established
- persistent language difficulties
- sensitivity and excessive reactions to noises and textures
- limited response to verbal instruction – children may be slow to respond and have problems with comprehension
- limited concentration, with tasks often left unfinished.

So what did our parents notice?

> 66 Matt's speech was unclear: he could not articulate certain words and found particular vowel sounds very difficult. He also used to make up words, so he would say 'unager' for biscuit. We later learned that some of his problems were caused by verbal dyspraxia which affects the muscle control necessary for speech. 99
> **Clare**

It is not easy for parents to identify dyspraxia. People often think of dyspraxia as affecting physical movements, but some children have a form that affects the brain's ability to process and organise information and this may not be identified until adolescence. Rupert's mother Emma recognised the problem before the professionals did because she had already seen it in other members of her family, but Clare did not identify the problem till later on.

> 66 *Despite the fact that I am a trained occupational therapist, it was my husband who first realised that Matt had dyspraxia. There were so many indications when we thought about it: he didn't like loud noises or being surrounded by lots of people.* 99
> **Clare**

Dyspraxic children used to be known as clumsy children because of their lack of coordination, but it is not quite that simple.

> 66 *Jake is an only child so I have nothing to compare him with, but I knew from very early on that he was having problems. He was very slow to do things such as doing up buttons, tying laces, catching a ball, riding a bike. He was so accident prone, we used to joke that he would fall over his own shadow.* 99
> **Tina**

The brain sends a message but the body does not always carry it out. Children with dyspraxia may have hit all the targets for sitting, crawling and walking but they may have done so rather later than expected. You might notice that they fall over a lot, bang into things and are clumsy. This is because they find it hard to coordinate both sides of the body. Some children find writing very tiring and complain that their hand, wrist, arm, neck or shoulder hurts because their fine motor skills are not developed sufficiently.

> 66 *Rupert held his pencil in an odd way and was always writing with his hand twisted over so he was writing back on himself.* 99
> **Emma**

Fact file: dyspraxia

- Dyspraxia affects up to 10% of the population and up to two per cent severely.
- Boys are four times more likely to have dyspraxia than girls.
- Dyspraxia sometimes runs in families.

Children with dyspraxia may have difficulty with:

- handwriting
- fine muscle control – they may be 'all fingers and thumbs'
- speech
- coordination
- timing
- rhythm
- spatial awareness
- sports and games
- learning to ride a bicycle
- swimming.

Things to look out for

Does your child consistently use one hand for writing, for using a toothbrush or a pair of scissors, or does he change his mind? Most children have become decidedly left- or right-handed before they go to school but children with dyspraxia may take longer. They may have what are known as 'midline crossover difficulties' and find it hard to pick up something on their left using their right hand. Dyspraxia does not affect just the limbs; it can also affect speech because the child's tongue and lips do not work together to say words. Does this sound familiar?

> 66 Rupert was never a very physical boy. He showed little interest in climbing up things, but it was at nursery school that the first signs of dyspraxia were noticed. They said that he was having difficulties holding a paint brush and thought he had coordination difficulties. He

did not develop pencil control so his handwriting was terrible. 🙶
Emma

Recognising dyslexia

Dyslexia means children can't spell, right? No: the word 'dyslexia' comes from the Greek and means 'difficulty with words', but it is not the same as a problem with reading or spelling. Like some forms of dyspraxia, it may start with speech problems.

> 🙶 *When Ben was in nursery they used to practise writing their names on cards and posting them and he could not do it. Ben started to stammer. We slowed down his speech at home and eventually the stammer went away but his problems with reading and writing began to surface.* 🙶
> *Sarah*

> 🙶 *Chloe used to stumble over certain words when she was speaking. When she was learning to read she found it hard to break words into syllables and just used to guess at unfamiliar words. She did the same thing with spelling so it was just gibberish.* 🙶
> *Linda*

Although children with dyslexia may struggle with reading and with breaking down words into their sounds, most of them do get there in the end. However, they will still have dyslexia after they have learned to read and are likely to carry on experiencing difficulties in a number of areas, such as memory and organisation, working with other symbol systems such as numbers and reading music, map reading, distinguishing between left and right, planning and writing.

The definition from the International Dyslexia Association is very clear.

66 *Dyslexia is a neurologically-based, often familial, disorder which interferes with the acquisition and processing of language. Varying in degrees of severity, it is manifested by difficulties in receptive and expressive language, including phonological processing, in reading, writing, spelling, handwriting, and sometimes in arithmetic. Dyslexia is not the result of lack of motivation, sensory impairment, inadequate instructional or environmental opportunities, or other limiting conditions, but may occur together with these conditions. Although dyslexia is lifelong, individuals with dyslexia frequently respond successfully to timely and appropriate intervention.* 99
International Dyslexia Association[7]

Dyslexia checklist

Dyslexia Action suggests that if the answer to most of the following questions is yes, it would be wise to seek advice.

- Is he bright in some ways with a 'block' in others?
- Is there anyone else in the family with similar difficulties?
- Does he have difficulty carrying out three instructions in sequence?
- Was he late in learning to talk, or with speaking clearly?
- Does he have particular difficulty with reading or spelling?
- Does he put figures or letters the wrong way, e.g. 15 for 51, 6 for 9, b for d, or was for saw?
- Does he read a word then fail to recognise it further down the page?
- Does he spell a word several different ways without recognising the correct version?
- Does he have a poor concentration span for reading and writing?
- Does he have difficulty understanding time and tense?
- Does he confuse left and right?
- Does he answer questions orally but have difficulty writing the answer?
- Is he unusually clumsy?

- Does he have trouble with sounds in words, e.g. a poor sense of rhyme?

If your child ticks most of the boxes, it is worth investigating further as these signs can point to dyslexia.

Fact file: dyslexia

- It is found in people from all backgrounds and all levels of ability.
- It mainly seems to affect boys, but girls can have it too.
- It is neurologically based.
- It tends to run in families.

The main problems are:

- poor phonological awareness: problems with rhyming, identifying sounds or matching sounds to letters
- poor sequencing skills
- poor auditory discrimination and memory
- poor short-term memory
- poor self-confidence.

The Rose Review and dyslexia

At the beginning of 2008 the Department for Children, Schools and Families (DCSF) commissioned Sir Jim Rose, former director of inspection at Ofsted, to carry out an independent review of the primary curriculum. His review of dyslexia, *Identifying and Teaching Children and Young People with Dyslexia and Literacy Difficulties*, was published in June 2009. It says that dyslexia does exist and defines it in the following terms.

- Dyslexia is a learning difficulty that primarily affects the skills involved in accurate and fluent word reading and spelling.
- Characteristic features of dyslexia are difficulties in phonological awareness, verbal memory and verbal processing speed.

- Dyslexia occurs across the range of intellectual abilities.
- It is best thought of as a continuum, not a distinct category, as there are no clear cut-off points.
- Co-occurring difficulties may be seen in aspects of language, motor coordination, mental calculation, concentration and personal organisation but these are not, by themselves, markers of dyslexia.
- A good indication of the severity and persistence of dyslexic difficulties can be gained by examining how the individual responds or has responded to well-founded intervention.

This definition is important for three reasons. It identifies dyslexia as a condition that needs more than just good classroom teaching, that it can be found in children of all ability levels and not just the most able, and that it is a continuum that may also involve other difficulties such as concentration and motor skills. There are a number of recommendations for schools and education providers:

- training 4,000 specialist teachers in dyslexia over the next two years
- boosting early identification (for example from Year 1) and effective intervention for pupils with dyslexic difficulties
- making provision for dyslexia-awareness training for existing teachers
- including more special educational needs training in initial teacher training courses
- acknowledging the need for specialist teachers and one-to-one interventions for severely dyslexic pupils.

What is especially heartening about the Rose Review is that it recognises parents' concerns and lays the groundwork for a new system which hopefully will be less adversarial than in the past. Sir Jim Rose recommends that:

- schools should build a positive dialogue with parents and provide relevant information for them

- primary schools should provide support for children with dyslexia at transfer to secondary school
- there should be helpline advice for parents and teachers.[8]

Dyspraxia **and** dyslexia

There is an overlap between dyspraxia and dyslexia and children may have both conditions. Only an expert can decide if a child has one condition or both.

A child who has both dyspraxia and dyslexia is likely to have these characteristics:

- left/right confusion
- limited concentration span
- clumsiness
- be a late talker
- be poorly organised.

Some children, especially those who share characteristics with children on the autistic spectrum, may have problems with eating and sleeping. See Chapter 10 for more information about this. The diagnosis a child receives may depend on the problem that is most evident at the time, whether that is language processing, coordination, reading or speech disorders.

Related conditions

Dyscalculia means having problems with numbers and spatial skills, both calculating and estimating. Typically children with dyscalculia will have problems telling the time, calculating prices and handling change, and measuring and estimating things such as temperature and speed. The International Dyslexia Association has suggested that 60% of dyslexics have some difficulty with numbers or number relationships.

Why are so many more boys affected?

Why do the statistics show that so many more boy than girls suffer from dyslexia, dyspraxia, Tourette's Syndrome, autism and other related conditions? According to Sebastian Kraemer, a consultant child and adolescent psychiatrist at London's Whittington Hospital, males are just more fragile than females and have more biological disadvantages. About 120 boys are conceived compared with 100 girls, but at birth the ratio has fallen to 105 boys per 100 girls, and by the time a boy is born he is likely to be six weeks behind a girl developmentally.

> 66 *Developmental disorders – such as specific reading delay, hyperactivity, autism and related disorders, clumsiness, stammering and Tourette's Syndrome – occur three to four times more often in boys than in girls, although girls, when they have such a disorder, may be more severely affected.* 99
> *Sebastian Kraemer[9]*

Left brain/right brain

You don't need to be a science buff to help your child, but a little understanding of how the brain works can make a difference to how you treat your child with dyspraxia or dyslexia. It will help you understand exactly **why** he struggles the way he does, and if he knows why he thinks in a different way, it can help to boost his confidence.

The two halves (or hemispheres) of the brain have different functions. The left side is really good at sorting and sifting information while the right side controls perception and intuition.

> 66 *Matt finds it hard to sift information and busy illustrations can be a distraction for him. The* Where's

Wally? *books where children have to find Wally in a crowded scene are impossible for him.* 🙺
Clare

While most of us use both sides of our brain, we have a bias to one side or the other. Traditional teaching works well for left-brained children with its emphasis on words, details and categorisation. The right side of the brain focuses on non-verbal and intuitive ways of working and is often seen as being 'more artistic'.

The left brain is good at . . .	The right brain is good at . . .
Being analytical	Being creative
Languages	Seeing the whole picture
Reasoning	Awareness of shape and patterns
Applying rules	Being intuitive
Mathematical formulae and numbers	Musical appreciation
Sequences	Flexible approaches to problems
Logic	Art

The majority of people have a dominant left hemisphere. This is neither a good thing nor a bad thing. While the majority of people are right-handed, it is not a disability to be left-handed. You just do things rather differently. So it is with people who are right-brained, as we shall see. Which characteristics come closer to describing your child?

Left brain	Right brain
Organised	Impulsive
Tidy	Untidy
Looks neat	Loses things
Makes lists	Spontaneous

(Continued)

A planner	A daydreamer
A worrier	Easy-going
Usually on time	Often late
Remembers birthdays of family and friends	Forgetful

Some people believe that most young people with dyslexia and dyspraxia have a dominant right hemisphere, but others believe that the problems occur because neither side is dominant.

Samuel Orton was an American doctor who studied children with learning disabilities just after the First World War. He found that many children who had problems with reading were ambidextrous or had cross-laterality, which meant that they might kick a ball with their right foot but write with their left hand. He believed that this mixed dominance was the root cause of many of the symptoms he frequently saw, for example confusing letters such as p and q and b and d, reading from right to left, reversing pairs of letters, and confusing words such as was and saw. Now there is more research showing that many, if not the majority, of children with dyslexia and dyspraxia are right-brained.[10]

> 66 Brain imaging studies are beginning to suggest that these difficulties may emerge in part because many children with dyslexia are endowed with a very strong right hemisphere that they use to read. In most people the left hemisphere is largely used in reading. The right hemisphere, which is involved in many spatial, artistic, and creative functions, is, however, very inefficient for reading, which would explain why it takes so long to learn to read. If this research proves correct, it also helps explain why so many great, creative figures have a history of dyslexia. 99
> **Maryanne Wolf**[11]

Compare Chloe, who has dyslexia and is creative and disorganised, with her brother Nathan. Nathan likes to have written directions to get from one part of town to another. If faced with a map he translates it into sentences: 'Turn right into Cole Street, second left and first right.' Chloe prefers maps. She loses the sequence of verbal instructions and gets lost.

> 66 *Chloe needs to see the whole picture before she starts studying. When Chloe went into secondary school she had some sessions on study skills using Tony Buzan's mind mapping. We got The Buzan Study Skills Handbook[12] out of the library and it made such a difference to her.* 99
> *Will*

You will learn more about Chloe's study methods, mind mapping and the Buzan approach on p115.

If your child has difficulty learning to tell the time, following instructions that involve left and right, learning the alphabet or with anything that has to be remembered in sequence, he is probably right-brained. He is quite likely to be artistic and creative but disorganised at times and impatient of fine detail. It is important that as parents we do not focus on the negatives: just because someone is dyslexic, it does not mean that he is not intelligent. Simon was assessed at the age of eight and found to have dyslexia and an exceptionally high IQ. At the age of 14 he is a member of Mensa. Sometimes we are just not clever enough to see where our children's strengths lie.

Why do children have dyslexia and dyspraxia?

The short answer is that we don't know. There has been a lot of research on dyslexia which indicates that there is a biological difference between the brains of children with specific learning difficulties and others. These differences affect the way in which they interpret information from their ears and eyes and how they learn new skills. It seems to run in families. Many parents report that they know of another member of the family with similar difficulties, and Keith Murphy, the behavioural optometrist you will meet in Chapter 12, agrees. When parents fill out his questionnaire about their child, it is not uncommon for them to realise that they have the same visual processing problems. You might like to cast your mind over your family and your partner's family. Are there others who have some of the same problems? Perhaps they dropped out of school early or avoid reading tasks or had problems learning their times tables. You may be surprised at what you discover.

Many experts say that there is no dyslexic or dyspraxic gene but a study by the Wellcome Trust Centre for Human Genetics in Oxford has found that several genes may be involved in dyslexia, although they are still trying to work out exactly how and why. The fact that there is no dyslexia gene as such, but several chromosomes have been picked out as having an effect, may explain why there is such a wide range of different symptoms and why some people are more affected than others.

The developing brain

A child's brain is fascinating, and when you learn a little about how it works you can understand more clearly why some children have specific learning difficulties. When a child is born, his brain contains 100 billion neurons. Shortly after birth, they start joining up. These connections are called synapses. They are the pathways that can be destroyed by head injuries, strokes and old age.

We know that the more a baby is talked to, played with and sung to, the more these connections fire up. In other words, nurture has a part to play in the development of the child's brain. However, what we are coming to realise is that, as children grow, the brain does an audit of the synapses and gets rid of the ones used least often, a process not unlike tidying up the hard disk on a computer to make it function more efficiently. It seems that children with dyslexia and dyspraxia do not lose as many synapses and so have more connections in their brain. Some years ago when I wrote a book about dyslexia for teachers I discovered more about this process.

> 66 As infants develop they go through a phase when many brain cells are destroyed. This is a normal part of maturation and results in the most efficient neural pathways remaining. For some children this reduction in brain cells does not always happen. Many more pathways remain and the brain has to make decisions about which pathways to use. This can lead to less efficient pathways being used and results in a slowness of speed and reaction time. It can also lead to clumsiness of movement or clumsiness in organising ideas (referred to as dyspraxia). 99
> **Supporting Children with Dyslexia**[13]

Think of it as travelling down country lanes rather than using motorways. As you might imagine, there are advantages and disadvantages to this. Thinking and planning are not so straightforward but there are lots more avenues in the brain for creative thinking. The children I have taught and the children in this book are often of above-average intelligence but they are 'different' and they are less consistent. Their brains light up like a Christmas tree while ours burn with a steady light.

Remember

- The terms dyslexia and dyspraxia are not absolutes; they both cover a range of symptoms.
- Not all children will have all the symptoms.
- There are many overlaps between dyslexia, dyspraxia and other conditions such as ADHD.
- It is worth looking at dyspraxia and dyslexia together in relation to your child.
- Use the checklists in this chapter to help you discover whether your child might have dyslexia or dyspraxia, or both.
- Many children feel they are different and lose confidence so you need to be extra careful to remind them of their successes and boost their self-esteem.
- Specific learning difficulties can run in families and affect far more boys than girls.

- Children with dyspraxia and dyslexia may be right-brained and absorb ideas and information in more intuitive ways. They may be very creative.
- Most infants go through a phase when the brain discards the least efficient neural pathways. Research indicates that this may not happen to the same extent in a child with dyslexia or dyspraxia so they may take longer to process information and they may come up with more unusual answers.

3

The early years
Giving your child
the best start

Children develop at very different rates. Some children can read their name at the age of three and be competent enough with scissors to cut themselves a fringe. Others are only just out of nappies. Children's development is not regular and linear but goes in fits and spurts. It seems that nothing happens for ages and then you notice that they have acquired skills and are really quite capable.

You may notice that a young child is not making the same progress as his older brothers and sisters or seems to find things harder than other children of his age. Perhaps a health visitor or nursery worker has talked to you about your child's progress and you are feeling anxious, or maybe you are worried and are trying to get someone to take notice. This chapter will take you through some of the key concerns parents often express when their children are young and give you some starting points for activities to focus on at home.

When will you notice that something is wrong?

In 1997 the Dyspraxia Foundation conducted a survey of its members and found that, on average, parents were aware of difficulties by the time their child was three but did not get a diagnosis of dyspraxia until the child was six and a half.[14]

However, not all parents will be alert to the signs.

> 66 When Jake was very little, he drifted off a lot. We discovered that he had glue ear and needed grommets so we just assumed that his loss of attention was because he could not hear clearly. 99
> Tina

Many of the early signs pass unnoticed. Chloe was born at 37 weeks and was in the special care baby unit with breathing difficulties. She also had a low Apgar score. This is the assessment carried out on new-born babies that measures heart rate, breathing, muscle tone, reflexes and skin colour. There were no problems until her three-year check-up when a health visitor noticed that she did not have the fine motor skills to thread beads, but this seemed a minor problem so no action was taken. However, a problem with fine motor skills can be an early indication of both dyslexia and dyspraxia.

What can parents do?

- If you are worried about your child's progress, make a note of any concerns so that you have everything in one place if you need to talk to a doctor, speech and language therapist or educational psychologist. Include a description of your pregnancy, information about the birth, where the baby was born, whether it was a full-term pregnancy, the weight of the baby and any comments from doctors.

- Make a note of the dates for lifting the head, rolling over, sitting and standing, walking and speaking. It's a good idea to do this at the time, but if you haven't, sit down with other members of your family and try to recall when these important events occurred.

There are new government proposals for a reform of the statementing process. According to the Green Paper on special needs, *Support and aspiration: A new approach to special educational needs and disability*, every child will have his or her cognitive development assessed by the age of two and a half. Health visitors will administer these tests and they might lead to early identification of dyspraxia. These proposals should come into effect by 2014.

Common problems for children with dyslexia and dyspraxia in the early years

Children with dyspraxia seem to react badly to the texture of certain foods (mashed potato, chocolate and fizzy drinks were all mentioned by our parents) and, as we all know, a baby's sleeping patterns can dominate family life. Children with dyspraxia seem to have more than their share of sleep disorders and share certain characteristics with children on the autistic spectrum. They can have highly attuned senses and can seem very inflexible.

> 66 As a little boy Simon was unhappy about moving from a cot to a bed and would stand at the top of the stairs and scream. To start with we used to pick him up and put him to bed and stay with him till he fell asleep but it made no difference, so then we would just let him fall asleep on the landing and put him to bed when we went up for the night. He still has to have his bed up against a wall so he can curl up with no danger of falling out. 99
> *Sofia*

Strategies that seem to work include having routines for meal time and bedtimes. These give children a sense of security and make the day flow more smoothly. Children need to know that night time includes getting undressed, cleaning teeth and listening to a story. If children know exactly what is going to happen and the order in which things will happen, then they feel more secure. But watch out: some children with dyspraxia will stick very rigidly to the 'rules'.

> 66 *Matt can be obsessive and for a long time needed me to sit in exactly the same place when I was reading his bedtime story and could not listen if I sat somewhere else. We instituted a reward chart.* 99
> **Clare**

Once again, remember that dyspraxia and dyslexia sit alongside other specific learning difficulties such as Asperger's Syndrome and it is not uncommon to find behaviours that are commonly associated with autistic spectrum disorders.

Priorities for nursery and school

If your child is lagging behind other children of his age, you will naturally be very concerned and want to make sure that he will cope at playgroup, nursery or school. It's a good idea to raise concerns with the staff before he goes. You might want to talk to your health visitor too. Children with dyspraxia and dyslexia may take longer to learn basic skills such as toileting or getting dressed because of poor coordination or fine motor skills.

Some skills are more important than others. At home, focus on priorities – speaking and listening, social skills and mobility. If children cannot catch a ball, jump or get up a climbing frame, it is not a major obstacle to their well-being. If a child cannot communicate clearly or walk downstairs it is.

Focus on key skills

Memory and communication activities

- Telling stories
- Paying attention and following instructions
- Learning rhymes and songs
- Using words to communicate
- Following sequences
- Remembering and talking about what he did yesterday, last week or on holiday

Physical activities

- Using the toilet
- Going up and down stairs
- Fitting actions to songs
- Walking and running
- Putting on and taking off clothes

Social and behavioural skills

- Obeying rules
- Controlling temper
- Understanding that no means no
- Turn taking
- Playing nicely

Making your child as independent as possible should be your goal. It is tempting to take him to the toilet, sit him up at the table, cut up his dinner, dress him and blow his nose for him. Remember, though, that you will not be there when he is at school and he may not be able to depend on others. So, when your child is about two and a half, you need to turn a blind eye to the mess and encourage him to have a go for himself. It is very important that you start building his physical living skills, and above all his confidence, in a safe, nurturing environment.

One of the best things you can do for your child with dyspraxia or dyslexia is to find a good local playgroup. Here you will find a bigger selection of toys than you could possibly have at home, especially big toys for climbing on or through, construction toys for building gross motor skills, and craft activities for fine motor skills. At the same time, your child is learning how to socialise, mix with new people and be part of a larger group.

Social and behavioural skills

Behaviour can also be a key area. It seems as if you have only just got past the terrible twos and then you are preparing your child for nursery and school. All children need to learn to be part of a larger group, but children who have specific learning difficulties and have difficulties interpreting information or process language more slowly may need to have things explained to them at home so that there is time for the messages to sink in.

Children who have language processing difficulties may give vent to their frustrations.

> 66 At this stage Matt really was an unhappy little boy. He did not make eye contact and his language problems got in the way of making friends. He was also chronically inflexible and had the most explosive tantrums if things didn't work out as expected. This can be very humiliating when it happens in public. 99
> **Clare**

If your child has speech and language delay you may be used to 'interpreting' for him. Encourage him to play with other children outside the family so he has a chance to develop new skills.

What about reading and writing?

Some parents get so anxious that they push their child into reading and writing before school starts, and for children who may have dyslexia or even dyspraxia this can be the worst possible thing to do. Readiness is important in learning, and if a child is not ready there may be a lot of unlearning to do later on. Help by building your child's attention and concentration and other underlying skills.

Handwriting specialist Amanda McLeod has worked with many children with dyspraxia and dyslexia. She advocates lots of fine motor skills work to help children develop dexterity and precision, which will be invaluable for handwriting, drawing and many day-to-day activities.

- Go for anything which involves the child using one finger and a thumb. Try sewing, pegging out dolly washing, jigsaws, games such as snakes and ladders, or turning out the contents of a purse or piggybank and standing the coins one on top of another.
- Practise dot-to-dot activities and drawing shapes such as circles, zigzags and squares, which will lead on to letter shapes.
- Get Stabilo triangular pencils – these are much easier for small hands to grip. You will find them in many high street shops and supermarkets.

Memory

Memory plays a critical role in learning, whether it's the alphabet, times tables or finding your way round a school. One of the key characteristics of dyslexia and dyspraxia is what is sometimes called a 'short memory shelf'. This means that the child's working memory is not as effective as it might be.

Try to give clear, simple instructions for everyday tasks and sometimes get your child to repeat back what he has heard so he fixes it in his mind.

> 66 *Simon was always absorbed in something else that was more interesting to him. He also used to put his clothes on in the wrong order, so he would have his shoes on and then realise he had no trousers. We had to get him to say out loud what he should be doing.* 99
> **Sofia**

Teachers often complain that children cannot remember a set of instructions such as take your coats off, hang them up, and come and sit on the carpet. They get two out of three. The more you build the memory shelf, the more prepared a child is for learning and reading. Singing helps with memory and can be a good strategy later on for learning times tables, quotations or key facts. Try songs with actions, such as 'Heads, Shoulders, Knees and Toes', and encourage your child to do the actions whilst saying them in his head.

Words

All children need to be read to, but if your child has dyslexia or dyspraxia, he is probably going to have to develop compensatory strategies. If children have problems linking sound and symbol and decoding words, or if they take a long time to write things down, they will need a good verbal memory, a wide vocabulary and a love of language to keep them motivated. Read to your child, every day if possible. Go for simple repetitive stories with a refrain that the child can join in with. Include songs, jingles and poems so children get used to rhymes and can anticipate them.

> 66 Chloe loved the Pugwash stories and Mrs Plug the Plumber and would join in, shouting: 'Send for Mrs Plug! When Mrs Plug was sent for, Mrs Plug came.' She loved songs and rhymes and often recalled catchphrases from television programmes or the refrains of songs she had not heard for some months. 99
> Linda

Children need to learn about letter sounds so they can make sense of phonics in the early years of school. A lot of this phonological awareness can be done at home by playing sound-based games. Get your child to find as many words as possible that rhyme with cat, dog or lamp. Include nonsense words too. As with all early years activities, make it into a game – the sillier the better.

You do not need to teach your child all the letters of the alphabet but it is useful if he can recognise the initial letter of his name and the sound it makes: 'That's a Jake j!' You can introduce children to the letters of the alphabet using plastic letters, friezes and alphabet books, but the best way is by using fridge magnets as children will play with them, touch them, move them around and start to absorb what the letters are and what sound they make.

Numbers and maths

Dyscalculia is a problem with numbers and is more commonly found in people who have dyspraxia or dyslexia than in the population at large. This is not to say that all those who have a form of specific learning difficulty will automatically have a problem with numbers – after all, Jake is studying A level maths – but it is a good idea to build up early number and maths skills.

People often confuse mathematics and numeracy. Numbers are very socially useful – phone numbers, adding up bills – but they are a very small part of the maths skills we all need. Physical activity can help us to develop a sense of time and an awareness of shape, size and distance that are invaluable pre-maths skills.

- Try playing with water, pouring it into jugs and cups. Have fun with jigsaw puzzles, walking to the park, handling plants and seeing them grow.
- By all means do some counting, but rather than trying to get your child to learn tables or do adding up at this stage, look at games and puzzles and pick out familiar numbers in the street or on parked cars.
- Shopping trips that include discussions about the number of tins and finding out which is bigger or smaller and sorting the washing by colour, shape or size are physical activities which will stimulate mathematical awareness.

Remember

- Parents sometimes notice the symptoms of dyspraxia long before the professionals do.
- Keep a record of all your concerns, with relevant dates for the milestones such as crawling and talking.
- Children may react badly to certain foods and with sleeping.
- Routines are good but some children with dyspraxia may become inflexible.
- Speaking and listening, social skills and mobility are pre-school priorities.
- Do not force your child into reading and writing before school but work on essential underpinning skills such as hand/eye coordination, memory, a love of language and an awareness of size, shape and number.
- You may want to make early decisions about how much time children spend in front of the television.

4

Settling in at school

The primary years

Many families feel a real wrench when their children start nursery or primary school. If you suspect your child has dyspraxia or dyslexia you will probably be even more worried about how he will cope. Will he manage in bigger groups? Will he be bullied? Will he manage to go to the toilet and make friends and learn to read and write? It seems an insurmountable list of challenges.

There are many things you can do to help your child at this stage of his life. Some children with dyspraxia and dyslexia are quite vulnerable, especially if they are aware that they have problems explaining things to others or going up and down stairs.

If your child is not used to being away from you, arrange for him to spend time at a friend's house so he gets used to short separations. Arrange for your child to spend some time with children who will be going to the same school so he has a few familiar faces in the new place. Visit the school and spend a morning there and talk to your child about the changes in a positive way. If you express doubts and anxieties he is sure to pick up on them.

Since school hours are shorter than those of nursery or family centres, you might have to make arrangements for after-school care too if you work.

> 66 *My dad used to collect him from school every night and then I would come home, cook tea and then start working with Ben on his reading and letters. We decided he would go to an after-school club. This would give my dad a night off and I could go and meet him.* 99
> *Sarah*

Remember that many children with dyspraxia and dyslexia have to work harder than other children to cover the same ground and so are likely to find the school day exceptionally tiring. Some children find school is very formal and they have problems sitting still and concentrating, while others expect to be able to do what they want when they want and resent the discipline of the school day. It is common for children to become more babyish at this time as they need reassurance. It is also common for them to have tantrums as they vent some of their frustrations: 'I've been good all day and I can't do it any more.' Give them a bit of special time each night after school, especially during the first term.

Realisation

Sometimes it is when children start school that their problems with coordination and concentration become apparent. For many parents the realisation that all is not well starts at the school gates when a child is in reception class. You might have had some concerns before, but, day by day, you start to have solid evidence that your child is just not making progress. The other children come out with new reading books in those clear plastic folders and your child is still on the same one. You know you should be asking him about his day, but no matter how hard you try your eye is drawn to 'The Book'. Against your better judgement, a certain unease or competitiveness creeps in. Why are these other children doing so well? So before long there is the nightly battle over reading. The child begins to sense that he is not quite up to the mark and tries to avoid the issue, while the parents are determined to help their child to catch up. The less the child wants to read, the more concerned the parents become and the more pressure they apply.

> 66 We read with her every night. In fact we all knew her reading book off by heart but she could not read it when she was at school. Chloe had been such a sunny little girl but she became very anxious and overeager to please. It was pathetic. The school was labelling her as a child who was not very clever and that was nonsense. She had such a phenomenal memory but it did not translate into schoolwork. 99
> *Will*

It's so easy to see the problem clearly when you are on the outside but it feels quite different when it is your child. Some mothers feel that the teachers and learning support assistants are not on their side. This is a great pity because the last thing your child needs is to be piggy in the middle.

Falling behind

> 66 Simon started quite well but after two terms he fell behind. The school thought it was because we were a dual-language household and suggested we spent more time speaking English. My husband lived with us at the time and did not agree so it was another source of tension, which didn't help. Simon always had work to finish at home because he was either not concentrating or had been taken out for bad behaviour. We also spent extra time at home reading, tracing out letters and sounding them out. It was a very multisensory way of learning and gradually it did make a difference. 99
> *Sofia*

Jake was set lots of extra work to do at home. If this happens, do talk to teachers because children with dyslexia and dyspraxia expend such a lot of extra effort at school that they will be very tired at the end of the day. Homework is not likely to be very effective in these circumstances and leaves less time for fun and normal home activities.

> 66 Jake's ability was just not reflected in his work. He was articulate but could not write it down. His reading was good too; it was his writing which let him down. The school did not think he had problems; they were happy with his progress and when he fell behind they said he was lazy. 99
> Tina

Time and again parents say that their child has been labelled as not making enough effort. This is so hurtful, especially when a child is working at home every night to catch up and still making no progress. If you are being told that your child is lazy or not trying, you need to go and talk to teachers straightaway, before your child develops an inferiority complex.

> 66 In the infants department, Jake's teacher did not show any interest in him but kept him in at break times and lunchtime to finish work. She also made him keep a diary at home and write an entry every night when he got home. It was heart-breaking. As soon as you gave him a pen he disintegrated. In his head, writing was associated with punishment. 99
> Tina

But some schools are excellent. Ben's school put all sorts of support in place. They provided a communication book where teachers and Sarah could note down any concerns. This works very well if you have a child who is not very communicative or who forgets all about school as soon as he is out of the door. Ben's school also brought in an educational psychologist very early on to observe him in the classroom. Not all schools are so conscientious!

Chloe had looked forward to going to school and her parents had no particular anxieties but it became a great source of worry.

> 66 *She was bright and sociable and had made lots of friends at playgroup and nursery, but once she was in reception class she started to get stomach ache every morning and did not 'feel well enough to go to school'.* 99
> *Linda*

If your child is reluctant to go to school, you need to have a word with the teacher. It may be that he is not settling in or making friends. Children who are not very confident may feel overwhelmed at school so it is crucial that you make sure your child has plenty of experience of playing with other children and mixing with groups before he starts school. For most children it is probably as important to be accepted by the class and to have friends as it is to get on well with the teacher. By secondary stage the teacher is less important, but at primary level children need to be accepted and valued for what they can do. Unfortunately children with coordination difficulties are likely to hold back the team so they are the last to be picked for sports, and children with dyslexia may not do well in team quizzes, not because they do not know the answer but because they cannot process ideas quickly.

Bullying

Bullying is very common in schools. Most children will be on the receiving end of a bully's attention at some stage in their school life. Bullying might be physical and involve hitting and punching; verbal, which is name calling; or emotional, where children are excluded or ridiculed. This is the hardest to deal with and is especially common where children are different in some way. Probably the best remedy is to have good friends who stand up for you, but often at primary school friends are fickle!

> 66 *Jake did not enjoy primary. He was never a naughty boy but internalised a lot. He really was quite isolated*

and, because he was kept in so often, the rest of the class knew he was different and avoided him. He was bullied a lot. Some of this was just the usual name calling, jostling, pushing, but they also threw stones at him. Once they stole his hat and threw it up in a tree. Unlike other children, he had no real idea of how to get it back. He didn't have naturally good social skills. He was quite naïve and often had no real perception of what was going on. It was as if he was afraid to make friends. 99
Tina

66 *Chloe had been picked on when she was first in primary school but seemed to change as she went up the school. She was put on a table with other children who found work hard and gradually became quite sullen and disaffected. She stopped trying at school because she did not believe she could do the work for herself and was regularly on report for bad behaviour.*

At first we were not too worried. We would tell her off at home but to be honest we were relieved that she had come out of her shell and wasn't so mopey. We felt she was testing the boundaries and would settle down. When we were asked to go and see the teacher about bullying we assumed that she was the victim so we were really shocked when they said she had been making another girl's life a misery. 99
Will

Like many other bullies, Chloe had been on the receiving end and had learned to dish it out. Often bullies have immature social skills and find it hard to make friends. They are often seen as having low self-esteem, which may be true, but certainly they are frustrated, anxious and insecure and also have a need to be in control instead of always being a victim.

But bullying is not inevitable, as Sarah's story shows.

66 *His friend Joe came round and was reading the name on the back of my car. He said: 'It's such an easy word!' When Ben said he could not read it, Joe said: 'Never mind Ben, you always do up my shoelaces for me.' They are still friends! Many children experience bullying if they can't read, but this was a village school with a real family atmosphere.* 99
Sarah

The school doesn't understand

Some schools are brilliant at coping with children who learn in different ways but many teachers are not trained to spot conditions such as dyspraxia and so the children flounder. A survey undertaken by the Dyspraxia Foundation shows that, prior to diagnosis, schools saw children with dyspraxia as being naughty, lazy or immature.

66 *Parents reported such attitudes as: the child is bright so will manage; the parents are fussy, over anxious, over protective or neurotic; the child has emotional problems; the child has poor eyesight; the child is lazy, a slow learner, below average or stupid; the child has behavioural problems; the parent could not accept that the child was not bright; the child is immature and unready for school; the child is disorganised and useless; the child is highly strung; the school did not know what to do with him.* 99
Dyspraxia Foundation[15]

Sometimes schools seem to make bizarre suggestions.

66 *Rupert did not develop pencil control so his handwriting was terrible. In Year 2, the school suggested that he might be left-handed and they wanted him to start again, learning to write with his*

left hand. I was not keen on this as he had spent three years using his right hand. 🍏
Emma

The teacher may lack experience and you need to be prepared to fight your child's corner. When Clare moved from Oxford to Cirencester she found that the new school was very negative about her son Matt. The class teacher was inexperienced and would only meet Clare if the special educational needs coordinator was present.

🍏 *Every night I would see the teacher's beckoning finger and would be called in to a catalogue of misdemeanours. They wanted to move Matt down a year group, which I refused to accept. They had not seen enough of his abilities to make that decision without proper consultation or assessment.* 🍏
Clare

Finally, it is worth noting that schools have a different agenda from parents. The curriculum and its targets are very important to schools and they are how their effectiveness is measured. This may lead to some interesting conversations between parents and teachers, as Clare recalls.

🍏 *There were some comical moments, though. When he was in junior school the PE teacher called me in to say he was really worried because Matt could not do a forward roll. I did have to say that this was the least of my worries and that it would not be high on my agenda!* 🍏
Clare

What help can you get?

Many parents complain that the school is not doing enough to help their child with dyslexia or dyspraxia. First you might want to find out about the special educational needs (SEN) policy. Next you might want to look at the statementing process, which is a more formal way of ensuring that children's needs are met. The whole area of SEN provision is in flux at the moment because of the new Green Paper, so I have included key points from this.

Special educational needs policies

All maintained schools, including city academies, city technology colleges, pupil referral units and early years settings that receive government funding, must have a written SEN policy. Children with SEN should have their needs met, ordinarily in a mainstream school (or early years setting), and should be offered a broad, balanced and relevant curriculum. The views of parents and children should be taken into account.

The governing bodies of maintained schools have a number of statutory duties:

- to decide the school's SEN policy and approach, setting up appropriate staffing and funding arrangements and overseeing the school's work
- to do their best to ensure that the necessary provision is made for any pupil who has a special need
- to ensure that teachers in the school are aware of the importance of identifying and providing for those pupils who have SEN
- to ensure that a pupil with SEN joins in with the activities of the school, together with pupils who do not have SEN, as far as is reasonably practical and compatible with the child receiving the SEN provision
- to report to parents on the implementation of the school's policy for pupils with SEN and notify them when SEN provision is being made for their child
- to have regard to the Code of Practice when carrying out duties towards all pupils with SEN
- to appoint a 'responsible person', who makes sure that all those who work with a child with a statement of SEN are told about the statement.

Special educational needs statement

The statement is a legal document issued by a local authority which establishes what your child's special educational needs are and, if they are sufficiently severe or complex, that it is necessary for the local education authority to take action. It brings together reports from the parent, the child's teacher, an educational psychologist, a paediatrician or doctor and others who are already helping your child, such as a speech therapist or occupational therapist.

This statement is proof of a disability and can help you to get funds and support. Parents can write to the local authority and request a free 'statutory assessment'. The local authority has six weeks to make a decision and it must comply with the request, unless, having examined the evidence, they believe it is not necessary. If the parents disagree with the local authority's decision they have a legal right to appeal to an independent SEN tribunal.

If the school is unwilling to support your application, you can get an independent educational psychologist's report as a parent or carer and apply for a statement. It is a good idea to involve the Parent Partnership, an independent body in each authority that works for parents. You may need a solicitor if you plan to take the school or authority to a tribunal to get a statement for your child or to get funding for your child to go to a special school outside the authority. If you need a solicitor, it is a good idea to consult the British Dyslexia Association, Dyslexia Action or the Dyspraxia Foundation for recommendations.

Remember
- Most parents of children with SEN are happy with the extra SEN support their children receive without the need for a statement.
- The process can take up to 26 weeks.
- Schools have to gather evidence. This can include medical evidence from speech and language therapists and educational psychologists as well as evidence from the school.

- Statements continue until the child is 16 but will be reviewed each year.

(See also Jeff Hughes's advice on p61.)

The Special Needs Green Paper

This is something of an unknown at the time of writing, but there are proposals for the reform of the statementing system. The Government intends that every child will have an assessment by the age of two and a half to identify those with special needs as early as possible and put support in place. Parents will be included in the assessment process and will have control of funding for the support of their child's needs. They will be able to choose which school they want their child to attend, whether mainstream, special, free school or academy, provided places are available. The key points are listed below.

- SEN statements will be replaced with an Education, Health and Care Plan, which will run from birth to the age of 25.
- School Action and School Action Plus (see below) will be replaced with simpler school-based systems.
- Teacher training and professional development will enable staff to work more effectively with pupils who are currently falling through the net.
- There will be greater independence in local authority assessments.

The Department for Education and the Department of Health are now working on a pilot project with local authorities and primary care trusts to trial the core proposals from the Green Paper: a single assessment process; the Education, Health and Care Plan; greater engagement of the voluntary sector; and use of personal budgets. The pathfinders, as they are called, are expected to work in partnership with those who deliver services for children with special educational needs. Those partners could include schools, special schools, academies and further education colleges, as well as those organisations that deliver health and social care services.

Quality First Teaching

You will learn more about diagnosis in the next chapter, but what is important is that a child starts to receive support as soon as there are indications that he is having problems. In the past a child would be assessed by a class teacher and might be identified as needing additional support; this might be School Action or School Action Plus, depending on whether the child's needs could be met in the main classroom or needed some extra input from a specialist teacher or a speech and language therapist (SALT). The child would have an individual education plan (IEP) which would be reviewed against targets to see if the provision was successful.

Now there is a move in schools to make teaching in the classroom more responsive to the individual needs of **all** children. You may hear the phrase 'Quality First Teaching'. This applies to all teaching, regardless of the age of the child, and has three basic principles.

1. **Multisensory and active:** All teaching should involve looking, listening and doing. Pupils need to be involved and engaged with their learning.
2. **Scaffolding:** Pupils are offered support through models, questions, prompts and dialogue. Support gradually fades away so they become independent learners.
3. **Metacognition:** Pupils learn about learning. They know how to motivate themselves, and they understand what a task requires and how to go about doing it.[16]

Many of the principles chime with the dyslexia-friendly classroom, but remember: Quality First Teaching is not specifically for children with dyspraxia and dyslexia. It is a policy to support all children, including those with behavioural problems, children learning English as an additional language, and gifted and talented pupils.

Achievement for All

Achievement for All (AfA) is an initiative aimed at the 20% of the school population identified as having special educational needs and disabilities or who are underachieving. It has been trialled in 10 local authorities with over 450 primary, secondary and special schools. It has three components:

1. improving the aspirations, progress and achievement of all children and young people, through high expectations, effective use of assessment and focused target setting supported and informed by:
2. improved engagement with parents of children and young people in supporting their child's learning through target-focused structured conversations, which:
3. improve the achievement, access and aspiration of children and young people and provide a wide range of learning opportunities in the classroom and beyond.

For parents of children with dyspraxia and dyslexia, the structured conversation may be the crucial element. Early indications from the trial show that where this works well, parents are happier with provision and are less likely to want to change school, and the number of referrals to a tribunal has fallen. It marks a change in the relationship between parents and teachers because schools have to receive as well as give information and must show that they have listened to parents about their child's learning.

Remember

- It is natural to worry about your children and how they will cope in the bigger arena of school.
- This may be the time when problems start to emerge, especially with concentration and early reading skills.
- Bullying can be an issue.
- Good friends and good two-way communication between home and school can smooth the path.

- The new Green Paper, Quality First Teaching and Achievement for All will hopefully raise standards and make classes more attuned to the needs of children with dyslexia and dyspraxia.
- Many schools take pride in supporting children who find learning more difficult than the average child. Talk to the school and try to form a positive relationship.

5

Getting a diagnosis

When it comes to your child, you are the expert. If your son or daughter does not seem to be hitting the early years' milestones at the same rate as other children and you are worried, then it is time to talk to someone. Diagnosis may be made at different ages. You will not have an assessment for dyslexia pre-school, but if your health visitor has identified that your child is struggling with physical skills she may refer him for further tests. Bear in mind that children develop at very different rates and it is important not to label a child if he is progressing normally, albeit slowly.

Many people believe that dyslexia cannot be diagnosed reliably before the age of seven, while others think that the earlier the diagnosis is made the better. This will vary in different parts of the country, but it is not uncommon to find that a child receives a diagnosis only in secondary school. What is important is that a child starts to receive support before a diagnosis is made.

Start with the health visitor and your doctor. Here you may hit your first obstacle. Perhaps your child is on particularly good form that day or your doctor thinks the discrepancy between your child's ability and the norm is not wide enough to cause concern. Also the symptoms may lead to different diagnoses, such as speech and language delay or attention deficit disorder (ADD). This is why it is a good idea to take your folder with all the notes you have made and a written summary of your concerns. This ensures that you will not forget anything and they can keep your summary to add to their own observations.

At the very least your GP should be able to arrange hearing and sight tests to rule out auditory problems such as glue ear or visual processing problems. This is the first step along the road to a diagnosis. You may find that professionals try to deter you by talking about the perils of 'labelling a child'.

> 66 My GP first said 'possible dyspraxia'; doctors since have said 'possible autistic spectrum'. I think you have to focus on the fact that they are what they are, as long as their needs are met. Then the label is not important. 99
> **mumsnet member**

It is true that some parents arm themselves with so much knowledge about learning disabilities that their children become the walking embodiment of a condition, but this is rare. What is more common is that parents have unrealistically high expectations of their children and compare their own child with the most talented readers in a class, and not with the average child.

So what else can you do? Read up on the subject: you will find plenty of books in your local library, but also join online forums where you will find parents who have already gone the distance and are willing to share their stories and expertise.

> 66 Read up enough to convince your GP that you know more than they do – they'll refer you up the food chain to a specialist soon enough. 99
> **mumsnet member**

Ask an expert

Educational psychologist Jeff Hughes[17] has helped hundreds of children with dyspraxia, dyslexia and related conditions. He advises parents who have concerns about their child's progress to gather their evidence very carefully.

> 66 *Prepare for the long haul by getting a large lever arch folder and putting in every piece of official paper concerning your child from birth weight, to immunisations, to reports from nursery. Keep a note of any complications, including any postnatal problems, events in infancy, feeding, growth and the dates when the developmental milestones were achieved. These would include sitting up unaided, crawling, standing, walking unaided, making sounds, babbling, talking, sleeping through the night, dry during the day, dry at night, potty trained, attendance at playgroup or other pre-school activities. Take this with you to all appointments. Make sure it is in a sensible order so you can find a particular sheet easily. Make sure it is kept up to date and never take any papers out of it! The folder gives a visual reminder to professionals that you have done your homework and should be taken seriously.* 99
> **Jeff Hughes**

Below he explains the stages of getting a diagnosis.

At what age/stage should a child be referred to an educational psychologist?

When they need to be! The earlier you identify children with specific learning difficulties the sooner you can tailor provision in school and try to maximise skills. Teachers, parents and children will have more time to overcome problems. Screening tools are available but they are not as useful as the observations of parents and teachers.

How do you get a diagnosis?

If you need a formal diagnosis, there are only a few routes you can use. A specialist teacher can diagnose some, but not necessarily all, aspects of specific learning difficulties. An educational psychologist can provide a full assessment but you may also need an evaluation by a speech and language therapist (SALT) to determine the extent to which communication is affected or, in the case of dyspraxia, by an occupational therapist (OT) who can assess your child's physical and motor skills.

If you go through your local authority the assessment is free, whereas a private assessment will cost anything between £350 and £700. Ask the school how long you might have to wait for an assessment. Some educational psychologists charge by the hour and children with specific learning difficulties may take a long time to do the tests and need rest breaks. Do ask if the educational psychologist is willing to go to court or a tribunal. Some will assess a child and produce a report but are not happy to commit the time and resources for longer legal cases. You may have to pay extra for them to attend the tribunal. Your first port of call to find an educational psychologist for a private assessment should be your local British Dyslexia Association or Dyspraxia Foundation group. Contact the head office to find details: www.bdadyslexia.org.uk or 0845 251 9002; www.dyspraxiafoundation.org.uk or 01462 454 986. You could also contact the British Psychological Society (BPS) (www.bps.org.uk) or the Association of Child Psychologists in Private Practice (AChiPPP) (www.achippp.org.uk).

> ❝ We had already had our oldest child assessed so I arranged to get an educational psychologist involved. He produced a report showing that Rupert had characteristics of both dyslexia and dyspraxia. ❞
> *Emma*

How can you prepare for the assessment?

Make sure you have your paperwork ready. Gather all your information in your folder, preferably with the most recent at the front. You may find it helpful to make a clear summary of:

- what you know
- what you have been told
- what you have noticed
- who has done what.

Make sure you keep this up to date. I had one mother whose child had complex difficulties and she had been to over a hundred appointments over several years. Each time she had to start again describing symptoms and her concerns. A one-page summary of your child's history can save a lot of time and makes sure that everyone you speak to has the same basic information.

Talk to your child. If he is young, tell him that this is a kind of game with puzzles to solve. With older children you might like to say: 'It is an interesting challenge with a serious purpose and you will know more about yourself as a result.' As educational psychologists we don't want children to do badly, so the more relaxed they are the better. Ideally, when we see your child he has had a reasonable night's sleep, is not especially worried about anything and has not just arrived from the sort of activities that get the adrenaline flowing. It is also a good idea to avoid foods with lots of additives for 24 hours before an assessment as this can affect the results. I prefer seeing children in a familiar place such as school or home.

What happens in an assessment?

Usually I will contact the school to find out how the child is coping with reading, writing and maths. In the case of a private assessment, an educational psychologist might ask the parent to obtain this information from the school. This information will provide lots of background and needs to be considered in conjunction with information from the parents. It is important to get a rounded picture of the child.

On the day of the assessment, I will meet the child and take them through a series of different activities to measure skills. I look at literacy and numeracy skills and do a range of assessments from the Wechsler Intelligence Scale for Children (WISC) or the British Ability Scales (BAS). Some of these are word-based while others use numbers or images and shapes. I will also look at general knowledge. I like to watch a child as he does the tests because, for me, the way a child approaches a task can be just as important as the scores. I need to know if a child is anxious or not focused or unable to sit still because that can point to other issues which need attention.

Getting the results

The educational psychologist then prepares a report. This should be a description of the child that both the parent and the school will recognise as being true. If the report seems wildly at odds with what you know about your child, you need to go back to the educational psychologist and ask them to explain. The report has three functions: to confirm, dispel and add. It should confirm what is known about the child and his progress. It might dispel myths such as 'he's not trying' or 'he's lazy', and it should add to the pool of ideas and strategies that can help the child, such as arranging for homework tasks to be written down by a learning support assistant or various forms of differentiation. If you are not happy you can ask for a second opinion, but you might have to pay for this.

The diagnosis is not about taking sides with a parent or a school. The school should be the parent's best ally. If they have overlooked the child or have not made good provision, then they need to improve matters and an educational psychologist's report can add to their knowledge of that child and help them serve his needs better.

Coming to terms with a diagnosis

When you find out that your child has either dyslexia or dyspraxia, you might feel relief. You already knew that your child was different and not making progress, now you know why.

You may head straight off to research your child's condition and talk to family, friends and experts and find out as much as possible, and you will probably have new strategies to work on. You may even feel a sense of triumph if you have faced indifference or opposition from the school: 'We were right – now the school will have to do something.'

> 66 *When he got to top juniors there was a task where all the children had to write a bit about themselves. I saw what Jacob had written and I cried. I couldn't decipher it and it didn't make sense. It was time to take action. I paid to get Jake independently assessed. They identified that he had distinct difficulties. The important thing for me was that I could physically take something back to school and say: 'Now will someone listen to me, please?'* 99
> Tina

Is diagnosis a good thing?

Diagnosis can put an official stamp on parents' concerns and if your child has been struggling for a long time it can be reassuring. It can also help the child to get on the right track at school and not be dismissed as a nuisance. This is especially important for conditions that are less well known, such as dyspraxia. A diagnosis usually comes with a plan of action too. This can offer both home and school practical ideas of things to do.

66 *Ben was assessed by an educational psychologist in Year 1. He identified that he had auditory processing delays, difficulties recognising letters and forming sentences and suggested different strategies. He was on a scheme called Popat,[18] a phonics teaching for children with speech and language delay which helps them to break words into single sounds without using letters and without chunking or rhyming. He also did Fuzzbuzz,[19] a reading scheme based on phonic and high-frequency words.* 99
Sarah

A sample educational psychologist's report

Here is an extract from the educational psychologist's report for Chloe when she was nine and a half.

- Chloe should be encouraged to read for five to 10 minutes every day at home. She should also be given experience of paired reading in a situation where she can help a weaker reader as well as being in a situation where she can work at a similar level with a peer.

- In creative writing, Chloe should be encouraged to experiment with dictating a story to a tape-recorder. This will enable her to produce work which is representative of her ability to express herself rather than being limited by her ability to spell. She could then draft the story from the tape-recorder, using her word book or help from the teacher to spell words she is unsure of. The school might also experiment with a 'cut-up sentence' approach.

- Chloe should be encouraged to develop the speed of her handwriting. She has her own style of writing which does not seem to hinder her although she writes slowly. I would suggest that Chloe should be given speed tests to improve the fluency of her writing, and might use her spellings to practise this during the week in school.

- Chloe should be reassured that she is not in a remedial

grouping within her class. She has expressed some anxiety about this. She should be helped to understand that she may be in different groups for different work, as will other children.

Linda and Will had ambivalent feelings about the diagnosis.

> ❝ *We were devastated to learn that Chloe had dyslexia. It is not good news to find out that your child has a condition which is lifelong and is incurable. Up to that point we had hoped that it was something she might grow out of. However, we were pleased that we had so many specific things to work on. Chloe has never really come to terms with her dyslexia and hates being seen as different but she has evolved a host of strategies to deal with some of the issues she faces.* ❞

What if the diagnosis is not satisfactory?

Many parents remain mystified because busy professionals will sometimes give a diagnosis and a brief summary of different aspects but do not give parents a chance to prepare questions for a proper discussion. Michael Weber wrote an article in the *Evening Standard* in 2004 describing his experiences. Hopefully the situation has improved over the last few years, but his story 'The dyspraxia myth'[20] has certainly struck a chord with some parents.

The dyspraxia myth

'Forget about an academic education for your son,' announced the form teacher. 'He's not clever enough.' Unexpectedly, the annual parents' evening at the private school in north London, charging £3,500 a term, had become a nightmare.

'Send him to a low-grade secondary school and take him to an educational psychologist,' directed the teacher about my nine-year-old son.

'Why?' I asked, staggered by the startling directive.

'Don't you know? He's dyspraxic.' Bewildered by the middle-aged teacher's judgement, I wanted to ask a dozen questions, but the annual session was terminated. 'I haven't any more time,' she declared. After barely three minutes, I was dismissed from the room.

Michael Weber was not happy with the 'diagnosis' and sought further help and advice. Ultimately, he found that the assessment of his son was wrong.

'Yet far from being dyspraxic, by the end of four years my son was declared to be completely healthy and academically excellent. In the meantime, his self-confidence had been undermined, his education had been damaged and I had spent nearly £20,000 on a small army of private teachers and educational psychologists.'

Sadly, Weber's experience is not unique. There are many recorded instances of children who are told they have dyslexia and given intensive phonics work only to find that they have a sight problem. The moral of this is that parents need to use common sense and keep asking and checking.

Response from the school

Usually an educational psychologist's report will be sent to the school as well as to parents, and ideally the school and parents should meet to discuss ways forward. For example, the school may send a text to parents alerting them to homework tasks if the child is not taking work home.

However, even when they have an assessment from an educational psychologist, parents are sometimes disappointed by the provision they get from the school.

66 *We had Simon tested by Dyslexia Action. I found the report really helpful as it showed that he had a real problem with phonics. However, the school said they felt he was average in reading and writing and we had the impression that they thought we were the problem.* 99
Sofia

It's natural for you to worry about the educational future of your child at this stage. How will he cope? Should he move schools? Would a school with smaller classes be a better option? Does he need some type of therapy? Would a private tutor be a good idea? We will deal with the issue of school, and other options you may have, in Chapter 6.

Life at home

A diagnosis is just the start of the journey. Just because you now definitely know what's wrong doesn't make it any easier to live with. If a child has coordination problems and cannot ride a bike, for example, then maybe family bike outings are on hold. If a father is a keen sportsman and the child cannot catch a ball, there can be frustrations. These may be compounded if a younger child develops these skills naturally.

Once you have the diagnosis, talk to your child about it. Give it the proper name. 'You have dyspraxia and that means ...' However, depending on the child, it might be best to avoid specifics. If you tell a child he is clumsy or will have problems with reading and writing, there is an element of self-fulfilling prophecy. Make it clear that the label is not an excuse for bad behaviour or for not trying. Tell the rest of the family so they know that some of his issues or behaviours are not always in his control. There are some suggestions of how to cope with this in Chapter 11.

At this stage, many parents find it's a good idea to find support groups for their child. Jake found this helpful.

> 66 *He had started going to a local dyspraxia group where he met all sorts of children who had far more severe problems. Some had very poor speech and problems walking about. We also both read* Caged in Chaos *by Victoria Biggs, a girl with dyspraxia. She was 16 when she wrote the book and it is a brilliantly written account of what it feels like to have dyspraxia. He felt less alone.* 99
> **Tina**

A word about money: if you choose to put a child with special needs into private education (see Chapter 6), this has cost implications. Don't just think about whether you can afford the fees: think about what your other children might have to forgo – school trips and holidays? Will they blame their brother or sister if there is no money for the latest 'must have' technology? Will they feel different from their friends?

Fight the good fight

Those of you who are engaged in fighting the system, whether it is with medical professionals, the school or local authority, should contact the Dyspraxia Foundation (www.dyspraxiafoundation. org.uk) or the British Dyslexia Association (www.bdadyslexia.org. uk); they can put you in touch with local groups.

Another source of inspiration is *Guerrilla Mum: Surviving the Special Educational Needs Jungle* by Ellen Power (Jessica Kingsley, 2010). Ellen has two sons: Peter and William. Peter, who is 13, has Asperger's Syndrome, along with dyspraxia, ADHD, obsessive compulsive disorder, handwriting difficulties and some orthopaedic problems. William, who is 11, has been diagnosed with motor dyspraxia and severe verbal dyspraxia. He also has handwriting difficulties. After many years of fighting, Ellen has discovered that: 'The current system for meeting special educational needs favours those who have a diagnosis.' She advises getting a formal assessment and boning up on legislation, from the Disability Discrimination Act[21] to the SEN Code of Practice.

Ellen Power's story is testament to the fact that you need to stand out as a parent who knows what they are talking about and knows what their child is entitled to. 'Don't be afraid to show your knowledge,' she says. 'Those people with your child's future in their hands need to know you mean business!'

Remember

- Ask for help. Talk to the professionals and try to link up with other parents.
- Talk to the teacher and the special educational needs coordinator to find out what they know.
- Read up about the condition.
- Keep a lever arch file with copies of everything you find out. You might need to share it with teachers; you also might need it as the basis for talking to schools and professionals to get the right help.
- Find a support group: is there a local Dyspraxia Foundation group or British Dyslexia Association group near you?
- Talk to others in the same situation.
- Join an online forum – there are some good discussions on mumsnet.

If the school is not right for your child

Choosing the right school can be an art in itself. Parents often send their children to the school the local authority allocates because it is the closest to home and their children will be moving up with friends from nursery, primary school or middle school. However, parents have the right to state a preference for a school and can appeal against decisions (see Chapter 7). The choice of school is personal.

> 66 Children move to senior school at 12 in
> Gloucestershire and it was important to find the right
> school for Matt so that he could continue with his
> progress. I think you have to look at all the schools
> and go with your gut instinct of what is right for your
> child. One popular school was very nice but I felt it was
> too academic for him. St Edwards in Cheltenham is a
> Catholic day school and has been a good choice. 99
> *Clare*

School can be a sad and lonely place for a child, especially for one who is in any way different. Children may have unsympathetic teachers, be labelled as 'special needs' and picked on by other children, but, despite this, many parents leave their children where they are. After all, the child is settled and would miss his friends if he moved away. But sometimes something happens which is the final straw, or perhaps you are acutely aware that your child needs additional help. If you are dissatisfied with the support you and your child receive, write to the Chair of the Governors. Part of their job is to oversee the school's SEN policy and ensure appropriate staffing and funding.

Some of the parents interviewed for this book have left their child at the original school. Sarah left Ben at the primary school because it was a supportive and caring environment and he had many good friends there. Jake was not diagnosed until nearly the end of his primary years. He settled well at secondary school and has stayed on there for A levels. Chloe has not moved schools but intends to go to a further education college and sees this as a fresh start where she plans to leave her dyslexia behind. Helen had lots of private tuition and extra classes but left school at the earliest opportunity. However, Rupert, Matt and Simon all changed school and are happy with their choices.

What are the options?

It is a personal decision whether to opt for state school or private school, and there are advantages to both. Clare had a very unhappy experience with the state system and moved Matt to a private school.

> 66 This was amazing. In a few weeks he was a different child. He had an older teacher who was passionate about helping him to read and write and to find out how he learned. The teacher spent ages teaching him how to write a number 8. Matt drew it in different colours, made it out of play dough and wrote it in sand. 99
> Clare

It made a real difference to Matt that he was in a small class – 12 children with a teacher and teaching assistant – and that the school was freed from the rigours of the National Curriculum. There were fewer milestones and more time for individual teaching.

> 66 *His new teacher was also committed to getting him to read as soon as possible. She was convinced that once he got reading under his belt his confidence would improve and he would find school a lot more enjoyable. They used the Oxford Reading Tree and we did a book every single night until he cracked reading. Instead of the dreaded beckoning finger, we had a happy boy coming out of school clutching a book. He started to have fun at last.* 99
> *Clare*

Rupert's experience was the exact opposite. He started in the private sector but his parents found a local state school that worked much better for him. Emma had Rupert assessed for dyslexia. The educational psychologist made a number of recommendations but after a few months the school had not implemented these so they looked around for a different school.

> 66 *The school could not understand why he could write some long words very accurately but could not write a word such as 'was'. We were fed up with him being labelled as lazy and he was suffering from the teasing and bullying from other children. It was a private school and I felt there was little point his taking the Common Entrance exam because it would be very stressful for him and the local independent schools are not keen to take children with dyslexia or similar difficulties.* 99
> *Emma*

Looking for a new school

The severity of his dyslexia or dyspraxia may affect where your child goes to school. Some parents want a mainstream school because they feel there is a stigma attached to special education, but many children with specific learning difficulties really thrive in a specialist school because for once they are not different. Some parents believe that the independent sector with its smaller classes will offer more individual attention for a child who is struggling in a class of 28 children.

The Council for the Registration of Schools Teaching Dyslexic Pupils (CReSTeD)[22] is a good starting point for finding specialist provision. It is a good idea to visit all the schools that can accommodate your child's needs and then make your decision.

Questions to ask a new school

- Can I meet the special educational needs coordinator (SENCO)?
- How many children are there per class?
- How many staff are there?
- How many fully trained dyslexia teachers do you have?
- What proportion of the pupils have specific learning difficulties?
- What provision do you make for these children?
- What sports and PE activities do you offer? What do you have for children with poor coordination?
- Do you have a streaming system? Is it for all subjects or just languages and maths?
- Is there a separate unit for children with dyspraxia or dyslexia?
- If so, are lessons one to one or group?
- When children from the unit join other children for classes, how are they supported?
- What technology support do you offer?
- What about exam results? Do you offer GCSEs or alternative qualifications?
- Do you have a sixth form?

- If not, what are the options post-16?
- What do children go on to do when they leave school?

What about a private tutor?

You might want to think about hiring a private tutor. If your child is happy and settled at school you may not want to move him but you might want to get some extra support to boost his performance and help him to improve exam grades.

Tutors can also help with specific learning difficulties where the child is not getting enough support at school.

> 66 *We had Simon tested by Dyslexia Action. I found the report really helpful as it showed that he had a real problem with phonics. So we fixed up some specialist phonic tutoring and it really helped – so much so that he started to read quite happily. He was reading well beyond his age, although he was ridiculously choosy!* 99
> *Sofia*

Advantages and disadvantages

There are advantages to using a private tutor for children with dyspraxia and dyslexia.

- They can give specific help with spelling.
- They can offer intensive maths support where they start from absolute basics.
- They might offer one-to-one typing tuition for children who are going to be using a laptop for schoolwork and exams.
- They can help with exam techniques and show children how to make better use of their time.
- Individual tuition means no disruptions! This means that the child can concentrate better.
- Both parent and child can ask questions at any time so you can be sure that your child is getting a totally personalised programme.

- The sessions are totally child-centred and can be tailored to suit an individual student's learning style.
- Subject tutors can help with planning an effective revision programme for exams.

But some parents are reluctant to inflict more learning on their child.

> 66 Some mothers in my position resort to extra help and hire a private tutor, but children with dyslexia find school twice as hard so why give them twice as much? I wanted Rupert to remain a happy child. 99
> Emma

> 66 I had a private tutor twice a week who came to the house. She was nice enough but I resented it, especially when I was about 13. I just wanted to be like everyone else. I wanted to go to the shops with other girls after school or go back to someone's house and listen to music, but every Tuesday and Thursday I had extra classes with mum hovering on the stairs and checking up on us. 99
> Helen

How to find a private tutor

Word of mouth is probably the most common and the best way to find a tutor for your child. Schools tend not to recommend specific private tutors so it is best to ask other parents or friends. Many local dyslexia groups hold a list of specialist dyslexia teachers working in their area. You could advertise in local shops and search online. Typically tutors write about their experience and expertise, so you can search for someone suitable.

In all these cases, it is up to you to follow up a tutor's references. Ask for details of two referees, preferably the parents of some current or former students, and follow up with a phone call. Do not be afraid to ask for evidence such as certificates, but, ultimately, you need to trust your instincts. You know when you have found the right person to work with your child.

Alternatively you can use a tuition agency. Some agencies offer what they describe as a 'personal matching service' to find the right tutor to meet the needs of the individual child. You will probably pay an introduction fee and commission for every hour of study. Reputable agencies screen tutors, checking documents to ensure that the tutor is suitably qualified to do the job, take up references and conduct a telephone interview with would-be tutors. They may also look for an enhanced Criminal Records Bureau (CRB) check. As a parent you will also have the opportunity to discuss what your expectations of a tutor are.

Arrange a face-to-face meeting for you, your child and the tutor. Most tutors would not charge a fee for this initial consultation, but some might. Gather all the relevant information you need: exam boards, dates of exams, examples of the child's work, a list of concerns. Be realistic about what you expect the tutor to do.

Agree where the lessons will take place. Many tutors prefer to work in the student's home and may charge an additional amount for travel expenses. Working at home means that the child is more relaxed. Other tutors offer lessons in their own home, in which case you will need to take your child to the venue and reassure yourself that he will be safe. Trust your instincts, and don't be afraid of calling off the lessons if you or your child feels uncomfortable.

Home schooling

Many parents are tempted by the idea of home schooling. They feel that if children with dyspraxia or dyslexia are not making good progress at school or are unhappy or being bullied, then they would be better off at home.

Advocates of home schooling argue that since the home is a safe and happy environment in which to learn it will take away the fear of failure, behavioural problems and anxiety. This can be very beneficial if your child is anxious, lacks confidence and does not work well in larger groups. You can give your child one-to-one attention, and you know your child well so you can tailor the work to his particular interests and passions; this will undoubtedly increase motivation.

They also argue that, since home schoolers are exempt from the National Curriculum, they can spend time practising those skills that need reinforcing, so you can be sure that your child is getting time to work on spelling, handwriting and basic maths.

However, there are many disadvantages too. First, many parents are not trained to teach and do not necessarily know what level of skill and knowledge is satisfactory for a given age. Some parents do not do enough preparation and so lessons are pleasant but haphazard, with too much emphasis on instruction and reinforcement, reading and talking, but not enough on reflection, analysis and putting learning into practice.

Most parents cannot provide a 'broad and balanced curriculum'. Maybe they are strong on basic skills and sports but cannot do justice to science and history. Sometimes tensions from home spill over into the schoolroom, so what began as a battle over washing up affects the mood of the whole day. Recently the term 'hot-housing' has begun to appear on forums; this refers to those parents who provide every type of enrichment they can for their child, beginning in infancy, and schedule lots of extra events after school, at weekends and in the holidays.

Children with specific learning difficulties often have underdeveloped social skills. They need opportunities to mix with children of their own age and to learn how to get on with children with whom they have little in common. This is a key life skill, but what parent is going to invite uncongenial children into their home? Children also need to learn to be part of large groups and to find ways of getting the help and attention they need, instead of being given unquestioning support. This is a good preparation for university and the world of work and is hard to replicate in the more cosseted atmosphere of the home.

Think about how you will cope if your child does not make progress? Will you blame yourself or the child? How will these tensions play out in the home? Will it affect other family members? Finally, the most important disadvantage is that you are the child's parent. Children will have many teachers in their life – the television, friends, books, celebrities, role models and undesirables. They only have one family and that is the most important support you can give your child.

A Home Education (www.ahomeeducation.co.uk) has a section on children with dyslexia.

The virtual schoolroom

You might want your child to learn at home but feel you don't have the right skills, so you might want to look at some of the new online personalised learning and support programmes. These are individually tailored to the specific needs of each child and lead to above-average exam success.

Your child may work at home or in an inclusion unit, a pupil referral unit or a community centre, and uses a computer and broadband to join a virtual classroom. Here pupils use a headset to have a two-way conversation and they share the same electronic whiteboard as the tutor and other learners in the group. It has been used for a long time for pupils who have been excluded, for those who are too ill to go to school and for children with phobias. Now it is being used by some learners with dyslexia and dyspraxia. Some use it as a long-term alternative to school; for others it will be a temporary measure until they are re-integrated into full-time school.

Accipio Learning is one of a number of companies that offer a virtual school experience. It works in partnership with schools and local authorities for specific children at Key Stages 3 and 4 who cannot attend mainstream school for one reason or another and paves the way for some to return to mainstream education.

There are 25 hours of specialist teaching per week through live, interactive lessons.

Over 130 authorities have bought seats on the Accipio programme. A seat comprises a package of five GCSEs (or equivalents) and provides access to live classes taught online.

The advantages of the virtual schoolroom

- Removing face-to-face contact and group pressures can help children concentrate on lessons.
- No one child can dominate as the tutor can 'pull the plug' or mute those who are too disruptive.
- The first half-hour of the lesson is entirely interactive, with most of the learning taking place visually.
- All notes are provided so there are none of the problems associated with copying off the board or from a book.
- Children don't have to use handwriting. All work is typed so it is legible.
- If children need to revisit or revise a lesson, everything is filed in the 'library'.

It seems that some learners flourish in this environment and reinvent themselves without the weight of teachers' expectations or the pressures of their peer group. Once they stop being the worst in the class at reading or writing they can try being a different person, and for some it really works. Last year Accipio had a 98% pass rate at GCSE (grades A*–G) with 41% at grades A*–C. The problem may be getting the local authority to agree that it is the right solution for your child.

Remember

- Some children do not fit in at their school and are unhappy.
- State schools may have better special needs support and less pressure to achieve; private schools may have smaller classes and no National Curriculum.

- Tutoring can benefit children with dyspraxia and dyslexia and help them to catch up.
- Home schooling provides a safe environment with an individualised learning programme but there are fewer opportunities for children's social development.
- With home schooling, tensions may spill over into family life if a child fails to make satisfactory progress.
- Virtual schooling is another form of alternative provision that is offered by certain local authorities.

7

Teenagers, the secondary years and beyond

It is a big moment when your child goes to secondary school. While most parents worry about how their children will cope, it is also a great time for celebration. Look at all the things your child can do now that he couldn't do even a few months ago. He will have come through his Key Stage 2 assessments, developed very pronounced likes and dislikes, and found lots of ways of coping with things he used to find difficult. Often children think that everyone else will be super-confident and clever, so if they are feeling anxious about going to secondary school, remind them of all their achievements.

Many children with dyspraxia have found the book *Caged in Chaos: A Dyspraxic Guide to Breaking Free* (Jessica Kingsley, 2005) very comforting as it makes them realise that they are not the only person who has felt this way. Here is Victoria's description of her first day at secondary school.

> 66 *Class sizes were too big and I couldn't put names to faces. I had to take legible notes quickly and write down my homework and hand it in to the right person at the right time and remember my PE kit and look people in the eye when I spoke bring extra notebooks instructions to follow not fall over on stairs concentrate listen carefully too much thoughts in head hurting . . . and I also had to be more sociable, which isn't easy when you feel as if the space between your ears is clogged with thick porridge. 99*
> *Victoria Biggs,* Caged in Chaos

Plan some special celebration for the end of the first week so you all have something to look forward to. Make sure other members of the family, such as grandparents, are on board to phone up and take an interest in all the changes that are happening. Make sure they know to be upbeat and positive. If children think that you think they can cope, they seem to become more robust.

Preparing for secondary school

You will probably worry about how your child will cope with moving from one class to another, dealing with lots of different teachers, new subjects, new classmates, perhaps travelling to school by bus for the first time, and whether he will be lost in a sea of new children.

First of all, find out if the new school knows about your child and his difficulties. Most secondary schools have good links with their feeder primary schools and so children may already have been to open days, made some visits and spent a full day in their new class. If not, ask the school if your child can visit and talk to older children at the school before he starts there. Talk to the special educational needs coordinator (SENCO) at the primary school to see if records will be sent automatically to the secondary school.

Usually the secondary school will have someone who is responsible for transition; they liaise with the primary schools in their catchment area and spend several days in each school. They may come in and see the children working and may bring the Senco from the secondary school to meet children who will need extra assistance. Provision varies from one authority to another, but ask if there is a transition summer school for children who are working below their chronological age in literacy and numeracy. These generally last for two weeks, are very focused and intensive, and have provided a real confidence boost for many children.

> 66 Rupert is now at a secondary school where he has half an hour of individual support per week and can use the breakfast club and a home base where he can chill out. 99
> *Emma*

Sometimes a new school means a fresh start and pupils may have a battery of assessments in the first term. This can be a bit unnerving for children who do not cope well with pressure but sometimes it can be very revealing. Chloe, for example, had always been on what she called the 'thickies' table' in primary school for maths, but when she was assessed at the end of her first term in secondary school she was put in set four out of six. The teacher thought she had some natural ability but had been badly taught.

However, if you feel your child is not getting the attention he needs or that the school is not geared up to deal with a particular difficulty, you might need to intervene.

> 66 Jake went off to Arden School in Knowle armed with the knowledge that he was dyspraxic. I had written to the school and discovered that while they had heard of dyspraxia they did not really understand what it was, so once again I had to fight for some kind of recognition of his needs. Through the Dyspraxia Association I arranged for an occupational therapist to come into school. 99
> *Tina*

What can you do?

Quite often you will see questions such as this on internet forums: 'My child is due to go to secondary school and I don't like the one we have been allocated. What can I do?'

- First of all go to visit the school. Sometimes a school's reputation is not founded in fact. Some of the very best schools for children with dyslexia and dyspraxia may not be popular with parents who only look at league tables. Go and have a look for yourself, talk to teachers and make up your own mind.
- Ask to go on the waiting list for your chosen school because vacancies will be filled from the waiting list.
- Look at alternative schools that were not on your original list and see if you can apply to them.
- Start an appeal by contacting the choice adviser in your local authority for help.
- Download the free booklet from the Advisory Centre for Education's website (www.ace-ed.org.uk).

Independent travel

Travel can seem like a major hurdle if your child has been used to walking to school. Some parents drive their child to school each day, but for the majority public transport is the answer. Independent travel can be a worry for parents of children with dyspraxia and dyslexia. Make sure your child has practised the journey before term starts and maybe has someone to travel with for the first few days. It is also a good idea to find out the exact time of the bus in the morning and set an alarm in the kitchen so when he hears it he knows he has to head out of the door. This is especially important for children who have poor organisational skills or do not have a good sense of time or who cannot read a clock or watch. A bus pass is usually cheaper and more convenient than having the right change for the bus each day, unless you have a child who habitually loses his belongings. In that case, see if you can get some form of travel insurance or have a big jar of spare change and get the right money out before bedtime each night to prevent chaos in the morning.

The school bag

Getting the school bag organised is crucial. Children with specific learning difficulties may need to carry even more than other children – from dictionaries to calculators to voice recorders. Chloe developed good habits in primary school thanks to one section of the educational psychologist's report.

> 66 *Chloe should be encouraged to organise herself well for her work. She might like to produce a reminder checklist for herself, perhaps in the form of drawings rather than words. She could then check that she has everything she needs before she begins work and also re-check at regular intervals, such as at the end of a piece of work, that she has put things back where they will be accessible for the next lesson. I would suggest that Chloe should be encouraged to improve her organisation through the use of merit certificates and other incentives which the school may use. 99*
> **Educational psychologist**

This really paid off because Chloe used the same strategy when she went to secondary school. Instead of keeping track of pens, pencils and rulers, she now had sports kit, cookery apron, locker keys and calculator. Her mum helped her to make a 'to take' list for each day of the week and this was taped into the back of a notebook, along with spare copies at home and in her locker. That way she knew what to take with her to school and, just as importantly, what she should be bringing back.

Technology

> 66 *Matt has not really needed any special input although he sometimes needs extra help with instructions. He*

*does not perform well in exams and his handwriting is
atrocious but he will soon be getting a laptop.* 99
Clare

If your child has been assessed for dyslexia and handwriting and
composition have been highlighted as particular issues then he
may already be one of the lucky few to have a computer in primary
school. All children will be moving towards using a computer
for course work at Key Stage 4 and will receive training in basic
computer functions as part of their ICT classes. Some children
also receive touch-typing lessons and support for using mind-
mapping software when they get to secondary school. Some
schools also offer access to voice recognition software, predictive
software (which suggests words for pupils to choose from) and
text-to-speech software, which reads back what is written to help
with proofreading.

Get in touch with the Senco at your child's new school and see
what facilities will be available. Sadly, several of the schemes
which in the past provided technology for children with specific
learning difficulties, such as the Communication Aids Project and
the Home Access Project, have now finished and so there is less
technology available. Do not assume that a child with dyslexia or
dyspraxia will automatically have his own laptop at secondary
school. If you want more information about technology, look at
the dyslexic.com site, especially the section called Sharon's Corner
which is full of useful information for parents of secondary school-
aged pupils with specific learning difficulties.

Have a look at the hints and tips on ways of using technology in
Chapter 9.

Communication and
social skills

In secondary school, children will not be with the same group all
day and so will be mixing with many different people. Children

mature at different rates in their teenage years and those with dyspraxia tend to have less established social skills. I CAN (www. ican.org.uk), the charity that supports children in the UK who have speech, language and communication needs (SLCN), is pioneering work with secondary school-aged children because the communication needs of some pupils only come to light when they move to secondary school. They are running projects all over the country and campaigning for more speech and language work in schools. They maintain that speech and language problems lie at the heart of many behavioural issues and are aiming to make classrooms better places for children who have attention problems.

In primary schools, relationships are often quite physical. Children charge about and do things together, but adolescent relationships are characterised by talk. Some children find this difficult and do not blend in, either because they find it hard to compose thoughts in their head or because they use a form of language and a style of speaking that does not sit well with their peer group. Perhaps they talk in a rather grown-up, pedantic way so others think they are 'stuck up' or they come across as humourless and unresponsive so other children do not gravitate naturally towards them. This can make them very lonely in a crowd.

> 66 He always talked like a little adult and did not pick up on facial expressions very easily so he struggled socially. His social skills are a lot better now he is older. 99
> **Mother**

Alternatively, they may appear to be aggressive because they cannot engage in subtleties of language so they make bald statements that sound confrontational. Simon says the right things but in the wrong way.

> 66 At times his voice does not reflect the right intonation for what he is trying to convey so he can give the wrong impression. Despite being a good

> *reader, he doesn't read aloud well because his pitch*
> *and tone vary so much.* 🙾
> *Sofia*

Although he is very articulate, Simon's frustrations have boiled over at school and he does not always behave well at home.

We have already seen with Jake and Chloe in Chapter 4 that bullying can be an issue and it is quite likely to continue in secondary school.

> 🙼 *At first there was no great improvement. Jake*
> *seemed to make little progress and he was bullied again*
> *but Arden dealt with it very well, although he did not*
> *really settle and come into his own until the bully was*
> *expelled. At this point his confidence really grew.* 🙾
> *Tina*

Talk to your child, but remember to listen.

- Make time for your child to talk.
- Be alert to the things that he doesn't say as well as what he tells you.
- Does he talk about what he is doing at lunchtime?
- Does he mention friends?
- Does he seem short of money?
- Does he dread going to school in the mornings?

Schools are more clued up now and have a responsibility to do their best for children and to keep them safe and happy. If your child does not seem to you to be safe and happy, you need to tell the school. If they do not resolve the issue you may have to consider a different school or alternative forms of education. It is vital for children to find their feet socially, otherwise their academic work will suffer.

> 🙼 *The first year of secondary is about settling in*
> *and finding friendship groups. Rupert is happy and*
> *confident and that is what matters.* 🙾
> *Emma*

Keeping up with subjects

There is guidance on helping your child with different subjects at home in Chapter 8 but you may want to consider suitable options for GCSE as children go into Key Stage 4. By this time, you should have a clear idea of whether your child is academic, which subjects he likes and which ones he finds really hard. Certain subjects are compulsory – English, maths and science at the time of writing – but the school must provide you with access to at least one course in each of four areas. These four 'entitlement areas' are:

- arts (including art and design, music, dance, drama and media arts)
- design and technology
- humanities (history and geography)
- modern foreign languages.

Some children with dyslexia or dyspraxia ask to be exempted from languages on the grounds that they have enough problems with reading and writing in their first language and the orthographic system in other languages may confuse them more. This is a pity because children with dyslexia often do very well speaking a foreign language and get pleasure from being able to communicate well. If they are learning a language, such as German or Spanish, which has a more regular sound symbol correlation than English, they may find it surprisingly easy.

> 66 Jake was brilliant at history but there was too much writing and he avoided essay subjects. He was always good at speaking French but could not write it down. He did triple science and Chinese, which he found easier than French – his symbols were so much tidier than his handwriting. 99
> Tina

Many schools also offer practical or vocational subjects, which can be a great choice for some children.

> 66 *The school offers all sorts of opportunities and not just academic qualifications. Rupert will be able to do courses in dry-stone walling and other practical options which may suit him better.* 99
> **Emma**

Art, design and technology and ICT are often seen as subjects where people with specific learning difficulties excel. At secondary school there are so many different opportunities for art – from pottery to digital art to photography. Chloe has really enjoyed the range of art, music and drama at her school. Matt and Jake have shown an aptitude for maths and science and find these easier than subjects that involve writing, but other children really respond well to subjects with a strong narrative component such as history and literature.

Sometimes children need a bit of extra support at this stage because of the volume of work. We will look more at homework and study skills in Chapter 9 but there are different ways of helping children to keep pace with their studies. Chloe was struggling with the texts for English literature so her parents got the videos of *To Kill a Mockingbird* and *Macbeth* out of the local library and the family watched them and discussed them together. Once she had got the story in her head she coped much better. They also bought her a Kindle and she studied *Kindertransport* and *Animal Farm* using this. She liked being able to change the size of the font and used the text-to-speech feature when she got tired.

Exam concessions

When children do not have statements, schools cannot allow extra time in exams without the consent of the examination board.

> 66 *Jake is much better on the computer. He can use the spell checker and grammar checker and produce*

his course work on it so it is legible, but of course they still can't use a computer in exams, unless they have a statement. 💬
Tina

Applications for GCSE and A level exam concessions have to go to the exam board several weeks before the exams begin. Make sure the Senco has applied as it cannot be done at the last minute. Think about what your child should do with the extra time. Children can get very tired. If they have an extra 10 minutes per hour and two exams a day, they could be doing an extra hour's work. The main alternatives are to plan for a short break at the end of each question when they will shut their eyes and do relaxation exercises to clear their mind, to use the time for proofreading if spelling and phrasing are a problem, to read through the question underlining key words, or to spend longer at the planning stage. It is entirely a personal preference.

Where next?

Rupert is keen to join the army when he leaves school. Chloe has decided that she wants a fresh start and has opted for a BTEC course in performing arts at her local further education college. This is the equivalent of two A levels. She will be doing an A level in theatre studies too, so she will be able to apply for university if she wants to.

💬 *Jake decided to stay on at school. He is a creature of habit and is comfortable at the school. He was adamant that he wanted to stay; he knows the school staff and set-up, and he wants to do a degree in science. He is enjoying A levels although for the whole of the first term he was exhausted. It is such a big jump from GCSEs with lots of homework and lots of independent studying.* 💬
Tina

Going to university

It is very heartening that so many young people with dyslexia and dyspraxia now go on to university. You will want to make sure that they are fully prepared for this exciting new venture and that they are going to get the support they need. If your son or daughter is planning to go into higher education, find out if the school can offer advice. Some people start by finding a university that has a good reputation for working with students with specific learning difficulties; others choose their subject and look at courses that interest them and then factor in the support afterwards. There is no right way to do this but do use the expertise in the school – teachers and careers staff and personal recommendations. You may find that your local dyslexia or dyspraxia group can help here.

Use the internet as well to research what universities say about themselves and what students think of their experience. One of the most useful resources is the Dyspraxic Teens Forum (www.dyspraxicteens.org.uk). Type 'university' into the search box and you get some really good posts from young people who are at university or who have left recently. Another great site is Dyslexia at College (www.dyslexia-college.com), which is packed full of advice on how to approach student services, how to give a presentation, time management, how to take lecture notes and how to read a difficult book. The site is for people in the UK and the USA, so you will have to skim to find the parts that are relevant to our education system, but it is worth it as this is an extremely useful repository of information and will save you a lot of searching.

Disabled Students' Allowance

Financing university is a concern and your child may need additional support such as a laptop or voice recorder. The Disabled Students' Allowance (DSA) is a grant to help meet the extra costs students can face as a direct result of a disability, ongoing health condition, mental health condition or specific learning difficulty.

They help people with a disability to study in higher education on an equal basis with other students. The course can be full time or part time but must last at least one year.

The university or college must be a UK degree-awarding institution or a college that receives government funding and provides a course leading to a degree qualification or a private institution offering specifically designated higher education courses. The DSA is paid on top of the standard student finance package, is not means tested and does not have to be paid back. The amount you get depends on the type of extra help you need.

The DSA can help pay for:

- specialist equipment you need for studying – for example, computer software
- non-medical helpers, such as a note-taker or reader
- extra travel costs you have to pay because of your disability
- other costs – for example, tapes or Braille paper.

Remember

- Going to secondary school is a rite of passage and your child will need help to become more independent.
- There will be more pressure on your child's ability to organise himself and on his social skills.
- Help your child make the transition by ensuring that his records and any concerns you have are passed on.
- Make sure he visits the school before he starts and check out the bus route.
- Find out what help is available at the school.
- Make your child take responsibility for his school bag and bus fares.
- Make time for your child to talk. Listen out for the things he does not say. Be sensitive to any signs of bullying.
- Help your child choose options for GCSE.
- Find practical ways to support your child's studying.
- Help your child decide on post-16 options.

Tips and techniques

Improving reading, writing, spelling and maths

As a concerned parent, you will want to help your child with their reading, writing, spelling and basic maths. This chapter is packed with ideas of things you can do at home which will really make a difference. There are also lots of tips from our parents of things they have tried and what has and hasn't worked for their children.

> 66 We kept trying to do a bit at home, but not too much, but it was a chore for him. Ben would come home so tired having worked twice as hard as other children yet he would only have done half as much work and then we had to start all over again trying to help him to catch up. 99
> *Sarah*

You will need to put in some time on your child's reading book, but try to limit this to just a few minutes and look for other ways of developing skills.

Reading

Reading is a complicated skill as children have to track text from left to right, match letters and groups of letters with sounds, translate the print into words and sentences and then interpret the meaning. There are so many skills involved, any one of which can be difficult for children with dyspraxia or dyslexia, who may have problems with eye tracking or matching symbol and sound. So you owe it to your children to make reading as much fun as possible.

Some parents test their child. They don't mean to but it turns into a session where the child reads and the parent corrects. Hopefully the hints and tips below will give you some ideas of different ways to develop skills.

Find out what approach your child's school is using. Many schools now use synthetic phonics. Phonics means teaching the sound associated with letters or combinations of letters such as 'th' or 'sh'. Children are taught to use the smallest sound the letter makes so they see letter t and say 't' not 'tuh'. Then they learn to blend or synthesise the sounds to make phonically regular words. Supporters of synthetic phonics prefer children to learn the 44 sounds of letters or groups of letters before being allowed to look at books. They move on to high-frequency words later on.

See what the school suggests but also make sure you read together and enjoy books as you did before school days began. Choose books from the library together. Don't worry if the books look babyish; we all enjoy reading below our level of competence. 'Trashy novels' are a very popular guilty pleasure! Similarly, if the book is too hard, read it together. Read a page and get the child to read a sentence or two. If he gets stuck on a difficult word, just tell him what it is. Often 'context cuing' will help. This means that the child will work out what the word is from its context. This is a great step forward as it shows the child is reading for meaning and not mindlessly decoding words. The key thing is to get the flow going so the story emerges. Read a paragraph aloud together or start off together and gradually fade out your voice so the child is reading solo. Sometimes if the story is really compelling, they forget they are 'no good at reading'.

> 66 *Chloe used to enjoy 'paired' reading, where she and I read together. She would let me take the lead and echo the words. This took the pressure off. She practised her skills and enjoyed the story too. When she got tired, I would take over the reading for a time while she continued to listen to the story. When she was about nine we read* Deenie *by Judy Blume together. Some would say it was too old for her but we enjoyed it.* 99
> Linda

Ten tips for reading practice

1. Ten minutes per day, five days a week is enough. Short, sharp and regular should be your watchwords.
2. Play 'knock, knock'. The child reads, but knocks on the table for you to read a difficult word. Sometimes you find that they remember the word the next time it comes up in the story.
3. Reading is not just about books. Many computer games involve a lot of reading. Look at magazines and comics too.
4. For some reason, children like reading to animals better than to people and animals like being read to. Our cat is very fond of being read to and never corrects our pronunciation.
5. Try family games where you have to do some reading, such as Cluedo.
6. Look out for non-fiction books and things that tie in to TV shows. Boys may respond to Top Gear more than fictional stories.

7. Use technology. There are lots of good e-books for the iPhone or iPad and they come with animations which may help to capture a child's interest. The backlit screen makes reading easier for some children. There are also lots of talking books. Some feature Disney characters that appeal to children and help them improve listening skills.
8. PocketPhonics has been a useful app for children with speech and language problems and for those who are stuck in the early stages of literacy. Pupils can listen to letter sounds and match them to the letter.
9. Look in your local library for talking books that come with a printed text so the child listens, looks and learns.
10. Take every opportunity to read with your child and to let your child see you reading. There is little point banging the drum for reading if it is seen as being something boring that only happens at school. Read bits of adverts, cartoons or local news out loud.

Overlays

You might find it easier if you change the colour of the page when reading. There is more information about Irlen lenses and coloured overlays in Chapter 12 (see p161) but you might like to try buying a set of transparencies in different colours from a stationers and trying them out. Many people wrongly believe that a yellow transparency or printing in blue on a cream or yellow background will make a difference. The truth is more complicated. Different colours suit different people and I once had a student who worked best with purple text on a shocking pink background which gave me a headache after five minutes.

Writing

Amanda McLeod[23] runs a centre in London for children who are underachieving in English and maths. She is a committee member of the National Handwriting Association. I asked her about handwriting and touch typing.

What sort of writing should we be aiming for?

A clear, joined-up script. If writing is not joined up, the writing is slower as the pencil is lifted off with every letter, rather than at the end of every word. But you need to get the child to form letters properly because, at speed, incorrectly formed letters reduce legibility.

How can parents support handwriting at home?

Either choose a handwriting scheme (see the section on handwriting books in 'Further reading and useful contacts') or ask the teacher how they would like your child to form his letters. The National Handwriting Association has very good tips for handwriting, including on pre-writing sheets, speeding-up skills and how to hold pencil. Look at posture too. It is not just about developing muscles in the hand and finger strength. Have a look and see how your child is sitting. The body should be leaning forwards, with the weight on the feet and elbows supporting the body. The back should be straight. Talk to an occupational therapist or handwriting expert if you have worries.

What about pens?

By the age of 11 children in private schools are using ink pens and may need a special dispensation to use a non-fountain pen. In state schools there is more flexibility over the use of pens. Try a gel pen. This is like a roller ball but with a built-in cartridge.

If you want to improve a child's skills with a fountain pen, then you could try practising with a calligraphy pen because it is not very forgiving! If you use a fountain pen badly you will get blotches, but with a calligraphy pen you will find you cannot make a mark at all unless you hold it properly. I had one boy whose writing was virtually illegible and very childlike. His parents thought it was a permanent feature of his dyspraxia. Once he started using a calligraphy pen there was an immediate improvement and, after three months, he writes beautifully even with a biro. Perhaps the best testimonial comes from his classmates who constantly tell him that his writing is now the best in the class.

What about touch typing?

It is a good idea for all children to do a course. I hate it when they have done it at home because so often they have been left to get on with it and then are using the wrong fingers. If they are using the 'hunt and peck' style where they just use their index finger, they will be more inaccurate and also slower. It is very hard to undo bad habits and in some cases it is just not possible. These bad habits hold you back at speed.

How long will it take?

To teach the alphabet on the keyboard takes about eight hours if there are no motor memory problems. Then it will take a month to a year (depending on the amount of practice children put in) to build speed. Go slowly; go for accuracy and speed will come. Rhythm building is important as rhythm helps build speed. Once you have learned the keyboard there is no point using a computer program. Instead, copy type from a recipe book or use similar materials which have large print and lots of short sentences.

When should children learn to touch type?

A child with dyslexia will benefit from learning to touch type at around the age of eight or nine, but if children have dyspraxia the body dictates how quickly they learn and when they are ready. Children with dyspraxia seem to make no progress for ages and then soar. I remember one child who made little progress between September and December. Her parents were all for taking her out of class but I told them to hang on a little longer. She did nothing over the Christmas holiday but then by the end of January miraculously she was top of the group. That is not at all unusual for a learner with dyspraxia.

The benefits of touch typing

Amanda has letters from parents and children that show the true value of touch typing.

> ❝ Theo has been transformed by his session with you. He now uses his laptop at school and for his homework; he raises his wrists, gets quickly into a new document, saves his work and so on. You gave enormously practical advice to us about what equipment he needs, how to work effectively in the classroom and how to make templates for tables and written work. I was so proud of his first typed essay, which was of course neat, beautifully spelt, more detailed and coherently argued. He spent no time at all settling down to his work and found it much easier to review his thoughts and commit them to paper in such a legible form. ❞
>
> **Mother**

> ❝ As a child you may not think that touch typing will be helpful but I'm in Year 8 now and I have got to do loads of essays and projects which all have to be done on the computer. It will also stay in your brain for the rest of your life and so one day it could help you with your job. ❞
>
> **Theo**

Spelling

> ❝ Drill and practice spelling activities have never worked for him. He would do look–cover–write–check and I would test him and he could do them all. Then he would go into school the next day and they would have evaporated and he would get three out of 20. ❞
>
> **Tina**

At school Chloe failed to take off with her reading and was constantly being compared unfavourably with her older brother. She was given lots of drill and practice for spelling but never seemed to make any headway with spelling tests. Chloe's mum Linda has lots of great hints and tips for working with spelling.

> 66 I could not understand why her spelling was so bizarre. The words weren't even the right length yet she was doing loads of phonics work at school. I discovered she didn't understand about syllables so she would just guess at the whole word instead of breaking it into parts. 99
> *Linda*

Linda devised a game where she would say a word and Chloe had to tap out how many 'beats' it had. 'I would say how many beats are there in watch, music, tyrannosaurus, history, seventy? Chloe would tap out the beats. Then we moved on to look at vowels and that each beat had to have at least one vowel or a y.'

Linda also used a novel way of working on spellings.

> 66 We did all the stuff about look–cover–write–check but this did not work for Chloe. Then I read about some children who practised their spellings with their eyes shut. Chloe had just moved on to joined-up writing so I thought it was worth a go. It made a real difference on some words. She would write them three times with her eyes shut and it seemed to give her a sense of what the word should **feel** like instead of what it looked like. It's not perfect but her spelling is improving. 99
> *Linda*

Ten tips for improving spelling

1. Find the little word in big words:
   - together – he went TO GET HER so they could be together
   - sincerely – SINCE he is sincere you can RELY on him
   - look for the MAN in perMANent.

2. Make links in your head:
   - friend – FRIday is the END of the week when I see my FRIEND.

3. Mnemonics – a learning technique that aids memory:
   - BECAUSE – big elephants can always understand small elephants
   - single c and double s in NECESSARY– necessary is like a shirt: it has one collar and two sleeves
   - RHYTHM helps your two hips move
   - make up your own – rude ones are usually memorable!

4. Get with the program.
   - Find a good phonics program such as Nessy (www.nessy.com) or Wordshark (www.wordshark.co.uk), or go online with Mr Thorne Does Phonics (www.mrthorne.com).

5. Make a list.
   - Try to make a note of the words your child is using. It is better for children to learn to spell the words they naturally use in their writing. Make your own personal dictionary.

6. Buy an ACE (Aurally Coded English) dictionary.[24]
   - Children can look up words as they sound and then find the correct spelling. Another handy choice is the Franklin Collins Spellmaster, a hand-held spell checker that offers a Collins dictionary of phonetic spelling corrections with 180,000 words.

7. Get out the red pen.
   - Get your child to have a go at words he cannot spell and then get him to use a red pen to mark the bits he finds a problem. This makes spelling active and not something others correct for him. It's a good way of working through the spellings from school.

8. Talk to me.
   - Use a talking word processor. Some are free and work with Microsoft Word. Try ReadPlease (www.readplease.com) and BrowseAloud (www.browsealoud.com). Use them to practise spellings and rules, as the sound reinforces the spelling.

9. Use touch.
   - Fill a baking tray with rice, flour or sand and get your child to trace the word then smooth it over.
   - Use fridge magnets.
   - Get foam letters and build words on the side of the bath. Be warned: most children go through a phase of writing rude words. Comfort yourself with the thought that most of these are phonic!

10. See the word, say the word, sign the word.
    - Some children learn to spell through movement as it can help to stimulate their memory. Look at the British Sign Language fingerspelling alphabet at www.british-sign.co.uk. Sign the spelling as you say the word.

66 Spellings were done in the look–cover–spell way but that wasn't very effective as Jake could remember them all in the short term but had forgotten them by the time he had his spelling test the next day. Slightly more effective was taking each word from the list, spelling it and then using it in context. I would get him to write a simple sentence using the new word in context to see if that would imprint better and it often did, but sometimes you would have to remind him of

the context to get him to spell the word. I also used to do one or two silly sentences at the very end of our session incorporating all the words on his spelling list so that it would make him laugh and ease the tension of the homework. 🙮
Tina

ICT and spelling

It seems that children learn subconsciously through the patterns on the keyboard. It won't work if they use the 'hunt and peck' method of keying in text; it has to be proper touch typing. Encourage your child to use a spell checker on the computer; this will show correct spellings and can stop children changing perfectly correct words. Work hard on what a word starts with. If you get the right first letter it improves a spell checker's chance of suggesting the correct spelling.

Maths

Victoria Biggs, who wrote *Caged in Chaos*, an account of her life with dyspraxia, has described the problems with mathematics.

🙮 *A cocktail of short-term memory problems, poor spatial awareness and an inability to pick up on pattern and sequence means that dyspraxic people usually have a very hard time making sense of mathematics. Students with concentration difficulties can't sift through mounds of irrelevant information just to pull out one answer. Pupils with perceptual problems can't mentally picture shapes and spaces, making topics like geometry nothing more than a meaningless haze. Manipulating a compass that seems to have a deep desire to drink your blood, keeping numbers in neat columns, and remembering all the rules and procedure are all really difficult tasks.* 🙮
Victoria Biggs, Caged in Chaos

Not every child with dyslexia and dyspraxia has problems with numbers: Matt has turned out to be good at maths, especially mental maths, while Jake is studying A level maths. But others get stuck at the basics.

> 66 *Rupert is a quick forgetter, rather than a slow learner. He does not retain information and still does not know his tables, but neither does his older brother or his father for that matter so maybe it runs in the family. We need to find more strategies for maths because he is interested in science and I don't want him to miss out on this because of his maths.* 99
> **Emma**

As Emma says, forgetting is a major problem. The trouble is that maths is often an exercise in memory – from number bonds (3+2=5) through to formulae such as pi and Pythagoras. Many parents are not very confident about their maths ability but you can do plenty to help your child along with numbers; the great thing about working with numbers is that the more you do it, the easier it gets.

There are various simple, basic maths skills where a bit of practice at home can make all the difference and lay the foundation for schoolwork. With young children you need to make sure they can count and have some sense of the meaning of numbers; that four is bigger than one and that these are not just words. The Dyslexia Parents Resource website (www.dyslexia-parent.com) has some good tips.

For example, have a dyslexic child arrange 100 marbles in a long line on the floor. Have him place a marker after each 10. The child can then practise counting all the way through to 100. Teach tens by using a different coloured marble in place of the tens numbers so that they stand out easily. After that, the child can learn to count by fives. The counting of numbers by 10 and five will help the child immensely when it comes to multiplication and time-telling skills. Have the child count forwards and backwards.

Number skills

- **Number recognition:** Can children link the written numbers with what they say as they count? Do they know that 5 is five is ☺☺☺☺☺?
- **Sequencing numbers:** Can they get numbers in the right order? Which is bigger, 25 or 52?
- **Practising number bonds:** Get a calculator and encourage them to use it. The more you play with numbers the more the number bonds and tables stick.
- **Estimation:** Which is bigger? Which is heavier? Is this half as big again or twice as big? Is the shop 100 metres away or 50?
- **Money:** From coin recognition to shopping, show children how mathematics applies to real-life situations.
- **Time:** This includes the 24-hour clock and time management – there is more about this later.
- **Remembering numbers:** Do children know their date of birth and their home phone number?
- **Understanding:** Get children to talk through maths and how they think they might do a calculation. Sometimes the maths gets lost in the words. For 'take away three from 19', what would the sum look like?

66 *Chloe finds maths hard. She used to have problems recognising the difference between the numbers 12 and 21 and confused similar 'pairs' of numbers. We used a red pen to write the tens and a blue pen for the units and one day she just got it.* 99
Linda

Multiplication and division are the most difficult for children to master. It will make it easier for them to learn if they actually understand the concept. Dyslexia Parents Resource (www. dyslexia-parent.com) has some ideas. Learning the times table can be a stumbling block. Some children learn them by singing them to well-known tunes. In the same way that spellings need to be in context, times tables meant nothing to Jake until he used them to work out a sum. Just repeating tables parrot fashion became a string of irrelevant numbers; using them in a wider context helped him get a better handle on them.

Remember

- Basic skills are essential but do not let them dominate your life.
- Read together and do 'paired reading'.
- Use e-books and apps for the iPhone and iPad.
- Joined-up handwriting is more efficient than printing but make sure the letters are formed correctly first.
- Getting the right pen can make a real difference to handwriting.
- Touch typing needs to be taught properly. Go for accuracy and rhythm and speed will follow.
- There are lots of alternatives to look–cover–write–check when it comes to spelling.
- Spelling programs on the computer can help, as does touch typing so children learn patterns.
- Not all children with dyslexia and dyspraxia have problems with maths.
- With times tables, don't just chant them but use them so the child sees their purpose.

Learning skills, homework and exams

Learning how to learn is one of the most important lessons in life. There is so much stuff on the web about learning styles these days: visual, auditory and kinaesthetic, or looking, listening and doing. People often think that visual is the most effective: 'a picture is worth a thousand words,' they say. For some children this is undoubtedly true, but bear in mind your child's early learning experience. They learned to walk by looking, copying and trying (visual and kinaesthetic). They learned to talk by listening, copying and trying (auditory and kinaesthetic). So do not dismiss other approaches.

Children with dyspraxia and dyslexia do not necessarily learn in the same way as other children in your family. Simon, for example, has a really strong auditory short-term memory, perhaps because his early years were spent in a bilingual home. He just has to hear a poem and he can recall lines very accurately for a few days afterwards.

Chloe needs to see the whole picture before she starts or she gets lost in the mass of details. Jake keeps focused by working at home, asking for help when he needs it, while Matt prefers to get his homework out of the way at school.

> 66 *Matt usually does homework on his own. The private school system is very disciplined and children get into the routine of doing homework from a very early age. Sometimes he stays on at school for prep and does his homework there. He can be lazy but we have found that financial rewards are a great motivator for Matt.* 99
> Clare

Skimming and scanning

Children need to learn to skim and scan to pick up information. What is the difference? Skimming is running your eye over the surface to gather an impression of the content. It is what we do when we are looking along the shelves in a supermarket to find something to cook for tea or leafing through a magazine. Children with reading difficulties often find this impossible; perhaps they have irregular eye movements so their eye does not flow smoothly across the text. Scanning means looking for a particular item: looking down a bank statement to see if we have paid for the TV licence, looking for a train time or the cost of an entrance ticket. It is picking specific information from a mass.

Whenever your child has to read a chapter and make notes, encourage him to skim the chapter first. What's it about? It helps with reading if you read for a purpose, so you can help him to make up three questions about the content so he starts to scan for more specific information. This helps him to see the whole 'map' of the chapter and the signposts – the order of the material and how it fits together.

> 66 *Chloe had some study skills sessions when she started secondary school. A learning support assistant*

(LSA) spent time showing her how to create mind maps. These were the brainchild of Tony Buzan, a psychologist who has written many books about study skills. The techniques he suggested worked really well for her so we got The Buzan Study Skills Handbook[25] *out of the library. It was so good we bought our own copy. Not all of it works for Chloe but a lot of it is really useful. One of her techniques is to write notes on the text. Not very popular with teachers, as you can imagine, but marking the bits which are important and putting a question mark in the margin for the bits she does not understand makes a difference. Her LSA said it was about becoming an active learner.* 99
Linda

Another technique Chloe learned was to jot down everything she knew about a subject in five minutes. Sometimes your child does not know much, so encourage him to jot down what he knows and put some questions he will need to find the answers to. Instead of letting information wash over them, children become active readers and this keeps them more focused and alert. This is quite good for exam practice too. It is also a good way of stirring up the little grey cells and moving them on mentally from their cup of tea or PlayStation into a studying frame of mind. Once they have jotted down facts and ideas, they have started to think about the subject and hopefully to use some of the language associated with it.

66 *Before I discovered mind mapping, I could not plan. If we had to hand in a plan I would write the essay and then create a plan from it. I did not know what I was going to write until I had written it and half the time I left out really important stuff.* 99
Chloe

Tony Buzan has what he calls ten core memory principles. He believes that you need to use every part of your mind, especially imagination and association, if you are to make learning effective:

1. your senses
2. exaggeration
3. rhythm and movement
4. colour
5. numbers
6. symbols
7. order and pattern
8. attraction
9. laughter
10. positive thinking.

Examples of this are children who learn to count by putting raisins on the table and then eating them, and the actor who learns his lines by pacing the room and incorporating gestures, stressing key phrases for extra emphasis. Other examples include using coloured pens for headings or for highlighting key points, making up rude mnemonics for spellings, and using question marks and asterisks to pick out key points in a hand-out. The best way to help children is to talk about things they might do and show them tricks that work for you.

Making notes and planning

If your child has a major problem with writing, see if the school can help. One of the suggestions on the Eleven Plus Exams forums (www.elevenplusexams.co.uk) is the following.

> 66 *Where teachers use whiteboards or have electronic forms of their lesson plans, print-offs are given out, to avoid that awful copying from the board problem. This has been especially helpful in subjects like chemistry where tiny misspellings can create a **very** misleading result! Inside the front cover of each exercise book there is a word list. Each teacher can list up to five words at any one time that they want her to concentrate on spelling correctly.* 99
> **Eleven Plus Exams**[26]

Lots of people make linear notes: they start at the beginning of a chapter, spend too long jotting down the key points of the opening paragraph, get bored and give up. Here is where skimming, scanning and writing in the margins can help. The faster you get to the end, the more likely you are to have the whole picture. One good strategy is to use self-adhesive page markers that you can buy from any stationers and most supermarkets. These are small, brightly coloured sticky strips that you can stick to a page and peel off very easily. This means you can read the text and put a clearly visible marker next to a key passage without damaging the book. The main advantage is that you can read the text and then go back and work through your bookmarks so you are not stopping and starting and losing concentration.

See if work can be presented in different forms – audio recordings, webcam, oral responses – and help children find a method of note taking that works for their learning style. As we saw in Chapter 2, Chloe works well with maps where she can see all the parts in relation to one another, while her brother Nathan translates directions into words. That process of taking ideas and putting them into his own words helps to fix things in the mind, so encourage your child to put into words the key points. For some children drawings may serve their purpose better as they can focus on the content and not get distracted by spellings. Some children who are left-brained like to make a neat, orderly plan for an assignment; others will benefit from a mind map.

There is a mind map for Chloe's essay on Hitler on the next page. (It's a little neater than the original!)

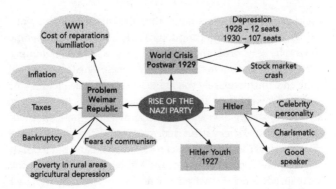

Why does mind mapping work? Again, it is about being an active learner. There is a mass of ideas and by putting them in different parts of a diagram and linking them together where appropriate, Chloe has imposed an order on them. Because she has decided on the connections, the plan is beginning to take shape in her head.

Composing an answer

Unfortunately you can't stay at the planning stage forever. Once the plan is made, the next stage is to write something, and this is where lots of young people flounder because they are worried about their handwriting, spelling and ability to get it down on paper. So what can you do to help? Emma has acted as secretary for her son Rupert; this is a good idea because it gets the flow going. It gives the child something to read back, which can trigger more ideas, and helps him overcome the fear of the blank page. Another good way of working is to get your child to put down all the headings and then dive in and tackle one of the middle sections. Again, as with note taking, people think they have to start at the beginning but then they get stuck, get disheartened and run out of energy. Motivation is a really important part of study and the best reward is to see something tangible for your efforts.

Concentration

Concentration is an issue for many of the children in this book. All children can be distracted or find it hard to get down to work but children with dyspraxia and dyslexia may lack the filters that other children have. For example, Simon can sometimes be almost obsessed by the ticking of a clock, which seems to drown out everything else in his head.

> 66 He responds strongly to stimuli and is exceptionally aware of what is going on around him. He was hypersensitive to noise when he was little and seemed to get sensory overload very easily. 99
> **Sofia**

All the families talked about how tired their children became.

> 66 He would come home so tired having worked twice as hard as other children yet he would only have done half as much work and then we had to start all over again trying to help him to catch up. 99
> **Sarah**

But interest and enthusiasm make up for a lot, as Tina points out.

> 66 Jake tires easily, especially if he is doing something which requires intense concentration. He can focus on something for about half the time of an average person but his concentration is amazing when he is engrossed. He can become fixated with things once his interest is engaged. For example, he read a book about the Battle of Agincourt and became obsessed with long bows. He soon knew all about their history, how they are made, and wanted to join an archery club. All this from a boy who would trip over a bow if we had one in the house! 99
> **Tina**

Learn to love your computer

Some teachers – and parents – still see the computer as something alien. They seem to think that children can move on to the computer once they have mastered handwriting and spelling. This is a great pity because some children will never get to a satisfactory level in these skills without a technological intervention. With a spell checker children are getting feedback about the words they want to use, instead of some arbitrary list set by a teacher. More importantly, it can stop them altering perfectly correct spellings. A keyboard can improve text output too.

> 66 The special needs teacher feels that it is pointless for Matt to spend hours on handwriting practice when it will never improve significantly. It is a much better idea for him to use a keyboard and produce legible written work. 99
> **Clare**

Amanda McLeod recommends using templates on the computer for longer pieces of work (see p105) and this can be a good way forward. If your child creates subheadings in Word 2003 on the PC for example, and then goes to the View tab and 'Document map', it shows a map of the document so he can write a section and then go backwards and forwards. (This will be different in other versions and on the Mac).

- To make a subheading in Word your child needs the Home tab. The styles are on the right-hand side. He will need to use the mouse to select the text he wants to be his subheading and click on the box that says 'Heading 2'.
- Perhaps your child might benefit from a dictation program such as Windows Speech Recognition in Windows Vista or Dragon Naturally Speaking 11 to input text. Be warned: dictation is quite difficult and it is not for everyone.
- Spell checkers can alert your child to spelling mistakes. Get him to look carefully at the suggestions they offer.

- If he is making the same mistake again and again, then he can right click on the spelling error and choose 'AutoCorrect'. Every time he gets the spelling wrong, the program will correct it. This frees him up to focus on the content. Too many children try to compose and spell at the same time.
- Go to the View tab, click on the 'Zoom' button and change 100% to 150%. This is great if your child has eye-tracking difficulties and is especially useful for proofreading.
- Change the colour of the text and page on screen. Go to the Page Layout tab then 'Page Background' and 'Page Colour' and pick a colour. To change the text colour go to the Home tab, select the text and choose a font colour.
- Make your word processing package talk! Use a program such as ReadPlease (www.readplease.com) or BrowseAloud (www. browsealoud.com) which will work with Microsoft Word. Your child can get the program to read back his work at the proofreading stage so he can hear if he has missed out words or written the wrong word. 'He leans very quickly' and 'the sun was shinning in the sky' are the sort of mistakes it is easy to overlook but are more likely to be picked up by listening.

Some schools recommend children to proofread by reading the work backwards so that they focus on each individual word. This is not a good idea for children with dyslexia and dyspraxia. They may have irregular eye movements. In fact, this can be the reason why they read slowly. Also, making your eyes move the wrong way along a line is very tiring.

Finally, a word of warning: parents should take an interest in their child's homework and check their progress, but some parents take it too far. Helen's mother took an unhealthy interest in her homework, as this example shows.

> 66 I remember we had to do a local history project where we went out of school and took lots of photographs of the local canal and how it had changed the area in the Industrial Revolution. I really loved this project and worked hard on it. My mum read it through

*and said: 'Really, Helen, you can do better than this.'
She got books out of the library and changed it all and
made me copy it out. It wasn't mine any more. The
teacher gave me a low mark. I think he thought I had
cheated. How do you explain 'My mum made me do
it!' when you are 15? It was easier to keep quiet.*
Helen

Revising for exams

*When Jake was revising he would just read it then
tell me he had done it. He did not have the skills to
rehearse or repeat and had no learning strategies
in place. He could not break what he had to do into
smaller chunks. His personal organisation was non-
existent so I sat with him for homework. He would do
some and I would test him. Then I would start him off
and go out of the room so he had to do more on his
own before I checked his work.*
Tina

Help your child decide where to study. For some people this will
be at home; for others the public library may be better, or an after-
school club. You might need to move a table into the bedroom for
a while. Wherever they choose to study, it needs to be free from
distractions. It is one thing to listen to your own choice of music
when working but it is not easy to focus when members of your
family are shouting at one another or have the TV on very loud.

*I am still not sure how Matt learns. We seem to have
long periods when he cannot do things and then it
stops being an issue.*
Clare

You can help children manage their time so they put in a good
stint but still have time out to watch their favourite programme
or listen to music. You might also want to cast an eye over any

revision timetable to make sure they have allowed enough time to cover all subjects. Make sure they have all the stationery items they need. This might include a hole punch, folders, a stapler and staples, index cards to note down important facts, lots of pens and pencils, highlighters, post-it notes and self-adhesive page markers for picking out key points in a text or an essay.

Encourage them to eat healthy food and not to overdose on snacks and drinks with additives and caffeine as these increase stress levels and cause dehydration. Some parents worry because their children stay up late studying. For some young people the night hours are the most productive, and while you would like them to get an early night they may be too keyed up to sleep. Talk to your child about this because children with dyspraxia and dyslexia do get very tired during exam season and may need more sleep, not less. Be careful how you phrase this. Children can be very irritable and touchy during this time. The YoungMinds Parents' Helpline advises: 'Try to work with your child and support them rather than "policing" them.'

Organising revision

Find out if there are revision sessions at school and make sure your child goes to them. Teachers are good at breaking subjects into manageable chunks. Look out for revision guides and surf the internet for study sites. Look at the University of Reading Study Advice site (www.reading.ac.uk/internal/studyadvice); it has lots of good ideas for making learning an active process.

> ❝ I also bought tons of revision guides and tons of notes. These are broken down into chunks so he can study and test himself. BBC Bitesize was really good. ❞
> **Tina**

If your child is having a particularly bad day, remind him of other useful strategies such as writing facts on index cards or post-its and sticking them in conspicuous places around the house. A change of medium might help. Some children find it useful to record their notes on tape and play them back to themselves. Making mind maps helps to organise and fix information, especially for those who have strong visual skills. If your child is still blocked, tell him to do as much work as he can, move onto something else for a while, and then come back to the problem topic.

Children are often told to plan but some have little idea what this means. Get them to jot down everything they know on a subject in five minutes using key words or pictures, then highlight the bits that would be relevant to particular questions. Parents can help with timekeeping and then get their children to talk through what would go in an essay. You don't need expert knowledge, just a watch and a sympathetic ear.

Ask an expert

Revision puts a lot of emphasis on memory. Jane Mitchell[27] is an expert on memory. A former speech and language therapist, she now runs a software company that teaches techniques for improving memory and helping children with their revision. I interviewed her to find out about the issues for children with dyspraxia and dyslexia and what parents can do to help.

Why do children do badly in exams?

Some students may not have had a good set of notes to revise from either because they missed lessons or because they found it hard to take notes. If this is the case, it is important to get hold of a set of good notes, from either another child or the teacher, or exam revision books so that your child has the correct facts to learn in the first place.

Because there are so many skills that are necessary to do well in exams, your child may need help with dividing what seems a huge task down into achievable bite-sized pieces, and will certainly need your continuing support and encouragement.

What about revision?

If you can recall the facts easily in an exam you can concentrate on applying them or writing a well-constructed answer, but if all your mental energy is dedicated to remembering the information you will not get good results. Some students don't do well in exams because they haven't remembered enough information. They need to start revising earlier for their next exams, to set themselves specific goals and maybe follow a reviewing system so they don't forget the things they learned at the start of the revision process.

How can you help your child memorise enough for exams?

Teach them to understand what works best for them. Some children do better if they speak out loud and don't just read silently. Singing facts along to a tune can also help get them into the memory. This is especially good for learning quotations for literature and history exams and for learning times tables too.

Once facts have been learned, will they go into their automatic long-term memory?

As much as 80% of information learned is forgotten within a day. So in order to retain information children need to keep reviewing it until it is securely placed in the long-term memory otherwise it may not be recalled under pressure.

How does reviewing work?

It might be re-reading or repeating the information. It might be more active, such as devising a test or getting someone else to test you. The first review should be about five minutes after they have finished revising to see whether the skill or information was really learned. Then review the information at intervals; preferably the next day, two days later, one week later and then at intervals until the exam. The old adage of 'a little and often' is supported by all the research on learning and is especially true for the revision of large quantities of information that is difficult to remember. Some children seem to learn well if they use a card index or a concertina file and physically move the information from one place to another once it has been reviewed.

Gearing up for the day

Once your child has an exam timetable, make several photocopies – one for the schoolbag, one for the bedroom, and one stuck somewhere noticeable like the fridge. Make sure the candidate number is on each timetable – this is information that you don't want to lose.

Get your child to draw up a list of equipment he will need for each exam; for example, Maths = ruler, pen, ink cartridges, spare pen, calculator, pencil, sharpener, rubber, crayons, compass, protractor. Tick the items as he puts them into his bag the night before the exam. Maybe he needs things such as plastic grips for pens and pencils, chunky colouring pencils, rulers with a grip on the top and colour transparencies.

On the day, provide breakfast and a snack that will not make a mess. This is not the time for yoghurt or cheese strings! Make sure he sets off in good time. Set an alarm or phone him if you are out of the house before him in the morning. Double-check the times of exams. It is not unknown for children to think they have an afternoon exam only to find that it went ahead without them in the morning.

Keeping positive

If children are nervous or have already experienced failure at school, you need to try to keep them upbeat. The YoungMinds Parents' Helpline says that parents should encourage their children to talk about their worries: 'Simply talking can really help to reassure them that if they do not get their expected grades, there will be other opportunities ahead.' The charity advises that this can be a tricky time for the whole family: 'While they are revising, children are often stressed, anxious and irritable, and can have trouble with eating and sleeping.'[28]

Your child	You
I don't know what to revise	Let's look at the plan you made
I can't work from my notes	Let's see if we can get you a better set of notes, or would you rather summarise the key facts on cards?
I can't do it	Have a five-minute break then review it again
I still can't remember it	Try another topic or subject and go back to it
I'm no good at remembering things	You are getting much better at remembering and you are learning new strategies all the time
It's all too much	You are doing so well and you can ask for help from other people. Is there anything you need today?
I expect I'll fail the exam	You are preparing really thoroughly so you stand a good chance of passing. If you fail you can take it again and you will benefit from all the things you have learned this time round. Remember: the best drivers are those who failed their first driving test.
I don't want to sit this exam	We're really proud of all the effort you are putting in and we will have to celebrate when you finish all your exams.

Remember: learning and homework

- Help your child to get the whole picture first of all before settling down to work on different sections.
- Help him develop skimming and scanning skills.
- Mind mapping is a very effective alternative to traditional note-making and planning techniques.

- Use colour, physical movement and humour among other things to help remember key points.
- See if the school can provide a copy of notes for use at home.
- There are three major learning styles: visual, auditory and kinaesthetic – aim for a mixture.
- Make good use of technology – the document map, subheadings, changing colours and fonts, and the zoom facility in Word.
- Use dictation software and a speech facility to make the computer talk if it will help.
- Act as a secretary for your child but do not take over.

Finally, here is a mind map for this chapter to show you what we mean.

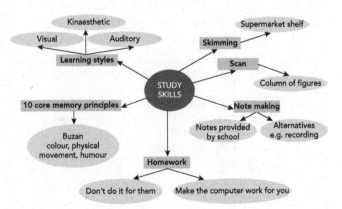

Remember: revising and exams

- Help your child find a good place to study.
- Make sure he has all the stationery, equipment and revision guides he needs.
- Cut down on caffeine and additives. These raise stress levels.
- Remind him that mind maps, recordings, drawing and singing can help with memorising material.

- Help with planning – both essay planning and making a revision plan.
- Find out about relaxation and visualisation techniques.
- Help him to review after he has revised so he keeps revisiting the materials and puts them into his long-term memory.
- See if your child is entitled to any exam concessions and make sure the school applies for them in good time.
- Keep positive.

10

Strategies for dealing with everyday problems

Home is supposed to be a sanctuary but sometimes it feels more like a battle station or pit stop where members of the family come for refuelling and running repairs. Time and again parents say their children are disorganised, and I am not sure that this problem is confined to children who have dyslexia and dyspraxia. However, while all children need to learn some basic life skills in order to become more independent, children with dyspraxia and dyslexia may need extra support for longer. The families featured in this book and on the web forums have turned up a host of useful ideas to make life more pleasant.

Tidiness

Sometimes it seems easier to tidy up after children than to train them to do it themselves but you are doing them and their future housemates no favours. Systems and routines seem to be the answer. First, you need to help them establish where things live.

Labelling drawers and boxes can be a very good system, but for children with poor memory or who cannot read try colour coding. Encourage your child to spend five minutes tidying up before bedtime. This has major benefits: the room is tidier, it is easier to find things, and it is safer if they sleepwalk or go to the toilet in the night. Also, the more often children tidy up, the more it reinforces their memory of where things should live. Train your child to use a large plastic box with a lid to keep vital documents in. This becomes more important as children get older and have to keep track of keys, glasses, bank cards, mobile phones, library cards, letters, university applications, forms and driving licences. At least it provides an effective 'dumping ground' when they tidy in a hurry and it gives them a starting point when they are looking for things.

> 66 On a bad day, the trail starts from the bathroom and continues across the landing into Chloe's bedroom and every surface is totally cluttered. She never puts the top back on things, so suntan lotion has taken the surface off her chest of drawers, some of her books were ruined when a can of Coke got knocked over and hair dye has ruined her carpet. To be honest, I don't see the point in replacing things till I know she is going to be more careful. 99
> Linda

Cleaning

Hoovering might prove dangerous for some children with dyspraxia. It is so easy to get wrapped up in the cord and go flying, but a carpet sweeper or a good old-fashioned dustpan and brush can keep the mess in check. Develop a routine for clearing and cleaning. Get them to put things away or place them in a carrier bag or box outside the door if they do not belong in the room. Suggest that they make it more fun by playing music or listening to a story or the radio.

Dressing

You need a speedy and orderly start to the school day so lay out clothes the night before; once your child is old enough, train him to do it. Lay out clothing layer by layer, with the underwear on top. If you choose trousers that are pleated at the front, it makes it easier to identify which is the right way round. If you get shirt collars one size larger than needed, they will be easier to fasten. Put a mark in the inside of the right shoe to make it easy to identify.

- School ties are a problem. You can do up a tie and then cut it at the nape of the neck and sew on Velcro so all the child has to do is stick the two ends together.
- Attach a house key or locker key with one of those long curly cords to trousers or waistbands.
- If your child is sensitive to light, buy lots of pairs of sunglasses and make sure he always has a set in his school bag.
- Make sure he packs his school bag the night before. He is less likely to forget vital things if he is not doing this at the last minute.

> 66 Rupert has trouble with laces but fortunately he has an understanding friend who helps him with his football boots so he is not always the last out on the pitch. 99
> Emma

> 66 Try to find clothes with fewer buttons. Matt has Velcro on his shoes and elastic laces in his trainers so he can just pull them on. 99
> Clare

Personal hygiene

Children with dyspraxia or those with dyslexia who have coordination and organisational difficulties can very easily present a very dishevelled appearance. Hints and tips for being tidy and looking good abound on the dyspraxia forums and in books. This is a collection of some of the best.

- It takes a lot of patience and good coordination to clean teeth effectively but a battery-operated toothbrush can make the job much easier.
- Nail cutting is a skilled job and can be tricky for dyspraxics. Try using nail clippers and an emery board instead of scissors.
- Going to the toilet can be a very tricky issue, and embarrassing for your child if it's something he struggles with. Some children have problems wiping themselves – this is something you can help them master. Try covering your child's hand with toilet paper and then guiding him so he gets to feel how to do it. Or try using wet wipes and sending him to school with a small pocket-sized pack so he can clean himself.
- For teenage boys, electric razors are an essential purchase when learning to shave and are best used with a magnifying mirror. They can also be useful for girls who choose to shave their legs, although some adolescent dyspraxic girls feel that shaving is dangerous and wax strips too painful, so depilatory cream is the only way to go.
- Encourage teenage girls to use sanitary towels rather than tampons. Go for the press-on towels without wings; the ones with wings seem to get stuck to uncoordinated fingers and cause a lot of frustration.
- Roll-on deodorants may be better than sprays.

> 66 Simon seemed to spray himself in the eye every time he used deodorant. I used to nag him for messing around but came to realise that he just had no idea where the spray would come out. He had a really sore eye after one accident so we moved onto a stick deodorant in a manly sandalwood fragrance. 99
> *Sofia*

Sleeping

Children need a good night's sleep if they are to function well but parents often say that sleeping is an issue. Some children with dyspraxia are super-sensitive to noise and wake several times a night. Both Simon and Jake have to have their bed up against a wall and Simon has to have heavy bedding well tucked in or he cannot sleep. Parents have found that aromatherapy – especially lavender oil – and blackout curtains are essential for a restful night's sleep. Others recommend ear plugs or listening to relaxation tapes.

Two of our families reported that their sons wet the bed right into secondary school.

> 66 He was always a restless sleeper and would wet the bed sometimes twice a night. We tried limiting the amount he had to drink but it made no difference. It seemed to do with poor muscle control rather than an over-full bladder. I found the ERIC site[29] good. I learned that one teenager in 40 still wets the bed regularly. He missed out on school trips and staying over with friends so it affected his childhood. We tried an alarm. It buzzed when he started to wet the bed and he would get up and change his sheet, but that was not a good idea because he could not get back to sleep. Afterwards, when he was 13, we got some tablets for him which he took for a month. Touch wood, they seem to have done the trick. 99
> *Mother*

Food

> 66 You decide to try a food and it's quite nice, but you can't eat it! Why? The texture in your mouth. For example, I don't mind the taste of lychee (a Chinese fruit) but I can't eat it because the texture in my mouth is gooey and gross! 99
> *Dyspraxic Teens Forum*[30]

> ❝ Most fruits I can't eat because of the fleshy texture,
> even if I like the taste. For example, I love orange-
> flavoured things, but couldn't eat an orange. Just
> about the only fruit I will eat by itself is an apple . . .
> Lastly, I can't stand chilli; if someone opens a jar on the
> other side of the room I can taste it. Definitely no need
> to eat one. ❞
> **Dyspraxic Teens Forum**

Children with dyspraxia seem to be particularly sensitive to
different foods, both to the textures and in some cases to gluten
or to additives. Other children seem to have no reaction at all.
Before you dismiss your child as a picky eater, keep a note of what
he eats and his reaction. For example, does his behaviour change
after eating certain foods? Do these foods contain additives?
The jury is out when it comes to diet. Some blame additives and
believe children do not function well for 24 hours after eating a
Chinese meal or foods containing gluten. Some children react very
strongly to a sugar rush or to soya, and in severe cases the child
appears to be intoxicated or high. Probably the best idea is to go
for a balanced diet with the same range of treats that any other
child would have.

Some children react badly to the texture of certain foods – mashed
potato was one that was mentioned several times!

> ❝ Matt was a fussy eater and now I realise he disliked
> the texture of certain foods. He could not drink fizzy
> drinks because he didn't like bubbles in his mouth.
> He could not use a knife and fork for ages and when
> we had family staying I could sense them looking
> down their noses when he picked food up with his
> hands. ❞
> **Clare**

Encourage your child to try new foods. Start with just a spoonful
and encourage him to mash it or mix it in with other things if the
texture is not to his liking. Packed lunches are probably a better

bet than school dinners. Sometimes children get better with food once they start cooking for themselves.

> 66 *Chloe wrecks the kitchen but I have to say she is a good cook. She did cookery at school and likes to experiment. She did a very nice Thai red curry recently for her dad's birthday and made him a fabulous cake.* 99
> Linda

Ovens are probably safer than hobs and a microwave is probably the safest method of all for children learning to cook.

> 66 *Jake enjoys cooking but is very messy. I cannot watch sometimes because I worry that he will have no fingers left. I encourage him to cater for himself as he needs to be competent when he leaves home.* 99
> Tina

Remembering things

Looking and listening are the key to remembering so encourage your child to focus and give you his full attention when you are telling him something important. Sarah discovered that one of the features of Ben's condition was that he could not do two things at once. In fact, few of his body skills were automatic so he found concentration very difficult.

One tactic is to get children to repeat back what you have said. Encourage them to adopt this as a strategy so they repeat things in their head too. Sometimes hearing your own voice can help to fix things in your mind. Some children work well if they can visualise things. If they have swimming the next day, they should try to imagine finding their swimming gear, wrapping it in a towel, finding a comb and shampoo, and putting the whole lot in a bag.

'To do' lists are what keep most of us on track. You don't need fancy stationery for this. Post-its or the backs of envelopes are fine. Again, as with the strategy of repeating things in their head, writing things down is an active approach and helps children fix the information more thoroughly in the mind. Children don't have to write in words; they can use pictures or symbols and stick the post-its on a wall or door. One popular exam strategy is to write a vital fact on a piece of paper and stick it to the mirror until it is learned completely. Of course, this only works if your child is the sort who looks in the mirror!

> 66 We have found that you need to avoid complicated instructions: keep things simple. Make sure they know what is happening and when. Structure is important. Avoid uncertainty. 99
> Clare

Time

Telling the time and judging time are two skills that seem to elude many children with dyspraxia and dyslexia. Partly it is because of the language of time. For example, we talk about ten to seven but this is 6.50, which has neither a seven nor a ten in it. Even worse, it might be 18.50! A digital watch is probably easier to use and a cheap kitchen timer with a buzzer is a very good investment. This can be set to go off after ten minutes, half an hour or any other interval so the child begins to develop concepts of differing lengths of time.

Finding their way

Even when problems with literacy, schoolwork and catching a ball have ceased to be significant, many young people with dyslexia and dyspraxia still have problems with navigation. They may find it hard to interpret directions such as left and right when under pressure (see Helen's stories of learning to drive in Chapter 13) and are often disoriented so they will set off in the wrong direction in a perfectly familiar building. On the forums there are some helpful suggestions.

> 66 *Sometimes I find it helps to remember landmarks in my head – often it's helpful to encode them verbally as my visual memory is dreadful. For example, I'll say to myself in my head: 'There's the bus station, then there's the Co-op and then there's the park.' So I'll remember the location of the park by first remembering 'bus station . . . Co-op . . . park'.* 99
> Charlotte on dystalk.com

Another suggestion is to use the map on a smartphone. This acts like a Global Positioning System (GPS) and shows a map as well as giving instructions, so if you have problems with left and right you can see on the map which way to go.

A word about contraception

Children will grow up and have sex and will not talk to their parents about it, so it is important that you talk to them in advance about contraception and also seek advice if necessary. If memory is a problem then maybe the pill is not a good idea. If coordination is an issue then condoms or a diaphragm may not be a suitable choice. Perhaps a contraceptive patch to be changed once a week, a contraceptive injection lasting three months or so or an IUD (intrauterine device) might be a better solution. This is a deeply personal issue but it is one that your children will face eventually so you need to be prepared.

Remember

- Personal hygiene is vital. Think about ways to make it easier for your child to look after bodily needs.
- Do not tidy up after your child. Help him to develop his own system.

- A good night's sleep is important for all the family. Think about bedding and put the bed by the wall. Invest in relaxation tapes, aromatherapy oils, blackout curtains, lavender pillows, etc.
- If your child wets the bed, try an alarm. Your GP can prescribe pills.
- Choose clothing carefully – Velcro saves a lot of frustration.
- Encourage your child to cook. A microwave might be a good option.
- Help your child develop better timekeeping skills.
- Help your child with strategies to find his way to unfamiliar places.
- Help your child develop better organisational skills with post-its and visualisation techniques.
- Contraception may be an issue in the very near future.

11

Dealing with daily frustrations and boosting self-esteem

No matter how hard you try, there will be times when life with your dyslexic or dyspraxic child seems to be an uphill struggle and it seems that the harder you try to help your child, the less you achieve. You might find that you are piggy in the middle, dealing with pressures from other children, your partner, maybe the extended family and perhaps your job. Of course, in these circumstances it is inevitable that you take it out on the people who are trying to help you and then you feel guilty afterwards, as Sarah found out.

66 *At this time I was very tired. I was working full time, coming home, helping Ben with work that had been*

sent home because he had not finished it in school, and then trying to do some extra reading practice. My dad had seen something about the Dore programme in Cardiff and said: 'Why don't you give them a ring?' It had been a very hard week and I was feeling so emotional, I just snapped at him: 'I haven't got time.' 99
Sarah

Balancing the needs of other children

The child with dyslexia or dyspraxia is not the only one in the family and you need to deal with conflicting demands. Many brothers and sisters feel that they get a lot less attention from their parents than their brother or sister who has dyspraxia or dyslexia. In some cases this is true. Even when parents do their best to share attention equally, the child with the greatest needs commands attention. This can lead to intense jealousy and resentment as the siblings feel that they are not as important or as special as their brother or sister.

66 *Josh got fed up with us. If he needed help when we were doing Ben's Dore exercises or wanted to tell me something or ask if he could go to his friends he had to wait. Sometimes he would storm off and there would be slammed doors.* 99
Sarah

They may feel they miss out on things because of their brother or sister. Helen had a very poor relationship with her sister until they both left home.

66 *Mum worried about me all the time and was always going on about the things I did wrong. I resented this but my sister Maddy resented me. She felt mum ignored her a lot of the time and that her problems*

were less important. I would have loved to have been ignored! 💬
Helen

Some of the features of the conditions, such as problems with reading and writing, clumsiness, being disorganised and being messy, can be an embarrassment both to the child himself and to his brothers and sisters. They may think: 'Why is he so babyish? Why can't he do more for himself? He's always clowning and drawing attention to himself.' It is important to remember that most children are embarrassed by members of their family and this has nothing to do with dyspraxia or dyslexia. Children are particularly embarrassed by their parents! However, along with feelings of irritation and resentment, brothers and sisters also feel protective.

💬 *Rupert is very easy-going and if someone punched him, he would not necessarily do anything about it. When he was in primary school and some boys tried it on, his older brother and sister had a word and dealt with it.* 💬
Emma

Children's frustrations

There are just not enough hours in the day for parents who are juggling jobs, home life, the needs of other children, fending off the school and then trying to coax the child into doing yet more work when he is exhausted from working too hard all day. It is an explosive combination, and, if that is not bad enough, some children can use the family as their emotional punchbag.

💬 *Simon plays mind games and has a way of drawing attention to himself all the time. He knows which buttons to press, especially when he wants to get a reaction from me. He enjoys upsetting his sister Molly, who is quite vulnerable. Meal times are a battleground and he is especially disruptive when other people are here.* 🙶

Sofia

Children with dyslexia and dyspraxia face so many difficulties in their day-to-day lives and must be encouraged not to give up. Parents can play a big part in helping their child to find alternative routes and methods to reach goals, but only if they are strong and calm themselves.

🙶 *Chloe is coping quite well now with her schoolwork because the school lets her do most of her work on a computer and she has developed lots of strategies which she has honed over the years. But she does get very tired. She seems to spend a lot of energy on having to organise herself during her day and comes home angry and frustrated. We often have a meltdown at the end of the school day. We used to call it her 5 o'clock shadow because it cast a shadow over the rest of the family.* 🙶

Will

Sometimes children with dyspraxia or dyslexia appear to be living in a dream world. If you ask them to do three things – clear the table, find the glasses and draw the curtains – you are likely to get only two out of three, and if there is a distraction that interrupts the train of thought, you might get only one. It is frustrating. Sometimes it looks as if they are avoiding their share of the jobs and that is no recipe for family harmony. A combination of working memory issues and problems with sequencing can have an impact on performance.

Wendy Fidler, a forensic education consultant, said: 'I know of a girl who was very bright, but had dyspraxia. She came back from university, went out at night, and her mum reminded her to lock the door when she came in. But in the morning it was unlocked. Her mum lambasted her and she burst into tears and said she'd forgotten the order in which she did it. She'd previously learned how to [lock up] by breaking it down into practical steps, but it went out of her head when she hadn't done it for a while.'

> 66 *People with dyspraxia can be extremely intelligent, but find physical movements and activities hard to learn and difficult to maintain, so they appear awkward and clumsy. They may not automatically pick up new skills, and need more repetition to help them retain them – even such apparently simple things as catching a ball or doing up buttons.* 99
> **Fiona Macdonald-Smith**[31]

Practical strategies for minimising frustrations

- Look out for 'flashpoints' and take action. Chloe's flashpoints are not unique and you might want to organise a time-out system where a tired child has a chill-out time before meeting up with the family or doing homework.
- Make sure the child – and you – has plenty of social opportunities to mix with others.
- Look for shared interests. These might include swimming, archery, martial arts, singing or photography. Go for normal activities rather than 'therapy'. Exercising on a Wii or using a dance mat offers a non-threatening, fun form of exercise.
- Encourage children to have a go and have some fun but try to avoid competition creeping in. It is good if each child develops separate hobbies and interests so that comparisons are irrelevant.
- Give clear, concise instructions and repeat these for the child if necessary. This is really important for things such as cookery where there is a lot of potential for mess.
- Try to find something positive to say: 'You started really well ...'
- Reward effort not achievement.
- Find what works for your child and don't worry if your methods differ from conventional wisdom.

66 *Matt still does not cope well with uncertainty. We have found that it is better to say no than to leave things open to negotiation. He needs boundaries, routines and structure or he becomes unhappy. He responds to targets and rewards. I promised him £5 if he got two pages of merits. It might not work for other children and some parents would see this as bribery (which it is) but it works and relieves the stress and improves domestic harmony. More importantly, it gives Matt an incentive to try things instead of shying away from them, and once he tries, he finds he can succeed. It helps to develop an upward spiral.* 99
Clare

Social maturity

Some children with dyslexia and dyspraxia seem to mature later than their contemporaries. It is hard to know if this is a feature of their condition or the result of the treatment they receive from family and school. Some children rely heavily on adults and seem reluctant to form friendships with their own age group. Maybe they hold back from the rough and tumble of social relationships which other children learn from. Sometimes it is their behaviour, their style of conversation or their body language which marks them out as being different. These mothers identified issues that affect their child's social skills.

- He still does not pick up on facial expressions very easily so he struggles socially.
- He does not read body language well and sometimes he will stand three inches from someone's face.
- He does not realise when people are bored or getting irritable and sometimes he is naïve about the subtext of things that are said on television.
- He needs a little more social maturity too. He doesn't always see how his comments might be interpreted; he takes things literally a lot of the time and is only just beginning to recognise sarcasm.

Sometimes children are natural loners and some parents report that their children seem to live in a world of their own or have better relationships online in the virtual world of Facebook than in the real world of the playground. Keep an eye on this and make sure they are staying safe online but do not condemn social networking outright. If nothing else, they are using and developing writing skills.[32]

We all want our children to be happy and have lots of friends but we need to let them find their own feet. Sometimes children will be excluded because of the things they cannot do, but if you stand back often they will develop their own strategies.

> 66 *When his friends came round they would often want to have a go on the games console and a lot of them were collecting sports car cards. Ben could not join in with them and it just underlined the fact that he could not read. So he would go out and kick a football about till someone came to join him.* 99
> **Sarah**

Children with dyspraxia in particular may not cope well with big groups and prefer to have just one or two friends. Lots of children with dyslexia and dyspraxia also feel that they are a disappointment to their parents. Helen felt this and it wrecked her relationship with her mother and affected her relationship with her sister for many years. You need to accept that your child is unique and special and not to be compared with others if you are to overcome some of those daily frustrations.

Self-esteem

Confidence will carry your child a long way in life. Every book you read about dyslexia talks about self-esteem. Most focus on the knock-backs that are commonly experienced by people with dyslexia and few tell you how you can improve a child's confidence. Let me start with a couple of examples from among my former students.

Jane had dyslexia and found spelling especially difficult. She persevered and went off to college to study art. She had a real inferiority complex and stayed in the same job for many years even though she did not find the work very satisfying. 'I feel a bit of a fraud,' she said, 'I have a degree but I keep thinking someone will catch me out so I never go for promotion and I'm not willing to go for a new job. They know me here and I can do the work. I might find it hard to cope somewhere new.'

Ricki was the opposite. He was quite accident prone, could not spell and was a very poor reader but he had a fabulous smile and oozed charm. He left school with a few GCSEs at grade E and walked into a job that called for much higher qualifications. His employer sent him to college to improve his literacy skills but Ricki spent more time chatting up the girls in the refectory. 'I'm definitely a Jack the Lad,' he said, and he was right. He had one great talent: he made people feel good about themselves. He never let his lack of qualifications hold him back and, last seen, he was part-owner of a gym and was enjoying more than his share of foreign holidays.

These are quite extreme examples but they do illustrate the importance of confidence. Some young people accept that they have some issues with basic skills but develop really good coping strategies, while others are so knocked back by the treatment they receive at school that they have an ongoing inferiority complex. One of the key targets for teachers at the moment is to encourage learners to develop independence. We have already talked about Quality First Teaching in Chapter 4. Part of the reason for this emphasis is that children can develop what is called 'learned helplessness'. They think 'Oh, I'm no good at writing' – so they don't try. You may recognise this at home when they say 'You're really good at talking to people so it would be better if you phoned them up' or 'Well, what do I put in a CV? Does this sound right? I don't know how to make it look good. What do I put in this section?' In the end you are (almost) tempted to write it yourself.

How can you boost your child's confidence?

- Nothing succeeds like success – try to find things they are good at and praise them for their achievements.
- Praise effort not outcomes: 'You really stuck at that piece of work. Well done.' 'You really have worked hard at that.'
- Be careful how you use 'but'. What you say after the 'but' is what people remember. If you say 'This piece of software is really very easy but it takes some getting used to,' the person thinks 'Oh no, it will be really hard and I won't be able to do it.' Turn it round to: 'This piece of software takes a bit of getting used to but you'll find it is really easy.' Suddenly the task looks manageable and there is implied praise.
- Sometimes people don't value praise from their own family. You can tell your child he is wonderful, clever and talented and it is meaningless. Let someone outside the family say 'You're not doing too badly at that' and it's as if the sun has started shining. It's just not fair! Try to find a family friend who offers a modicum of praise from time to time.
- Encourage your child to find interesting and absorbing hobbies that will give them a sense of satisfaction.

Valuing the individual

Many children with dyspraxia and dyslexia get great pleasure from their hobbies. They may not be a star at school, they may find social relationships a minefield, but they love things they do in their spare time for themselves. Rupert likes woodwork and things that involve him working with his hands. Chloe really enjoys acting and performing in musicals. Jake is drumming for a samba band and is now a workshop leader and tutor, working with younger children. Simon spends hours on iTunes. Ben is mad about rugby, which takes up his weekends, and he is now playing in a school team in secondary school. Matt's passions right now are collecting football cards, Lego, making little models, tennis, table tennis and cricket.

Many of the boys seem to like games of different kinds, especially military-type games where they can develop strategies and conquer the world. Sometimes this can be a solo sport but it can lead to social opportunities too.

> 66 *During primary school he had a little go on a PS1 and liked it so much I got him a second-hand one. It had enormous benefits in terms of giving him some common ground with other boys. He had something to talk about. Whereas others might talk about music or TV, he could chat to his mates about special effects, weapons, which level they were on.* 99
> **Tina**

Not everyone can be good at everything, but everyone has some talents. Here are some suggestions of areas where your children's abilities might lie. Some boxes have been left blank for you to add your own ideas. You might want to ask other people who know your child well to contribute ideas. Sometimes we just see the ugly duckling and don't realise it's a swan in the making!

Art and drawing	Acting and drama	Being independent	
Talking to people		Looking after animals	Making friends
Helping people	Sport		Speaking languages
Cooking		Being cheerful	Numbers and maths
Being persistent	Good eye for colour		Making people laugh
Playing computer games	Making money	Making music	Making models
Keeping himself amused for hours	Making up stories		Remembering songs

Looking fabulous	Working with people	Using the computer	
		Remembering facts	Playing with younger children
Sense of direction	Singing		
	Photography		Tidying up

Don't feel guilty

Sometimes you have just had enough. You feel you are propping everyone up and, like Sarah at the beginning of this chapter, there are moments when it all gets too much. Every family has its own way of dealing with conflict and annoyances but try not to bottle things up too much. Talking to your partner about problems may help but sometimes your partner may have a different stance and then you feel: 'Am I the only one who is worried about this? Am I the one out of step?' Try to see the funny side, although it sometimes takes a lot of imagination to do this! Make sure you have time for doing the things you like doing and keep in touch with friends; this will help you keep a sense of proportion. Many parents find that joining a local support group can be a lifeline. They say a problem shared is a problem halved and you might find someone has got just the answer to your particular problem.

You can find out about local support groups on both www. dyspraxiafoundation.org.uk and www.bdadyslexia.org.uk.

Remember

- Both you and your child will get angry and frustrated at times.
- Some children will take out their frustrations on their family. Set boundaries and encourage them to chill out somewhere on their own.

- Make sure brothers and sisters get their share of the attention.
- Children with dyspraxia and dyslexia can have immature social skills compared with others of the same age. Try not to worry. They will find friends!
- Boost self-esteem and find people outside the immediate family who can increase your child's confidence.
- Value the things your child enjoys doing.
- Make time for yourself and seek out the support you need.

12

Is there a cure?

Treatments and therapies

When you research dyslexia and dyspraxia one of the first things you learn is that there is no cure. Don't be downhearted! While it is true that these are lifelong conditions it is also equally true that with good teaching and support from home most young people will cope very well indeed, and, as they grow up, they will develop a host of strategies which will help them get round problems. However, there are a number of treatments and therapies that may help to alleviate some of the symptoms.

Many parents of children with dyspraxia will want to consult an occupational therapist who will assess a child's fine motor, gross motor, perceptual and sensory motor abilities. They can help children to develop specific skills, such as handwriting, or suggest different approaches such as using different pencils or trying a computer. They can also suggest simple adaptations to make life easier, such as using a chair with arms. You might also be referred to a speech therapist if they suspect language processing problems or if the child has significant communication difficulties.

We have already mentioned coloured lenses and overlays in Chapter 8 but we have a more detailed report here, along with information on other therapies. There are other treatments and therapies that at first sight appear not to be directly related to dyslexia or dyspraxia. Some of them are what we might call mainstream (such as physiotherapy or cod liver oil) while others are more unusual, such as catching bean bags to having the spine manipulated.

> 66 *I was desperate to find something for Chloe. I was convinced that if she had a more nutritious diet it would make a difference to her brain power. We cut out all sweets and anything with additives. She put up with it but she really kicked off when I gave her cod liver oil!* 99
> Linda

In the end Linda opted for a balanced diet, giving her the same sweets and treats as the other children had.

If you see a 'cure' you might want to try to get some answers on the forums or ask your doctor. Remember, even if it is a very reputable treatment, it might not work for your child. Here are some of the most common ones.

Physiotherapy
Theory

A physiotherapist will assess your child's motor skills and take a detailed history before devising a plan with goals and objectives. The aim is to improve the child's motor development, which in turn will raise self-confidence and esteem.

Evidence

A Three Year Study on the Progress of Children Following Physiotherapy Treatment for Dyspraxia by Michele G. Lee and

Professor Graham N. Smith is on the Dyspraxia Foundation website (www.dyspraxiafoundation.org.uk). It is a survey of 60 children who were followed up three years after the original treatment.

Drawbacks

You may be on a long waiting list for treatment unless you pay. It might take a lot of sessions before you see an improvement. You will probably need to supervise activities at home too.

Verdict

Reports show that physiotherapy has an impact on gross motor skills, self-confidence and social skills. However, there is less impact on schoolwork, mathematics, writing and short-term memory.

Have a look at www.dyspraxiafoundation.org.uk and search for physiotherapy.

> 66 We started to look at getting Jake physiotherapy to see if it might strengthen him and help him operate better. He has floppy muscles and poor posture. They discovered that he has no arches so the physiotherapist got him a referral to a podiatrist and he has implants in his shoes which he has to wear all the time. 99
> *Tina*

The Listening Programme

Theory

Children and adults with dyspraxia and dyslexia often have auditory processing problems. Sound therapy based on the Tomatis method of listening therapy can reduce the problems.

Evidence

Canadian research was positive. Professor Howard A. Stutt of McGill University said: 'The Tomatis APP [audio-psycho-phonology] approach to the treatment of certain problems of some children with learning disabilities seems to produce benefits beyond what could be expected by maturation or remedial education alone.'

Drawbacks

The programme consists of eight CDs that are listened to over an eight-week period. They have to be listened to through high-quality headphones using a good-quality personal CD player. Listening takes place for five days followed by two days' rest. The programme is only available through a trained, authorised provider. It costs up to £1,000. Alternatively, some practitioners offer sessions at £35 per hour.

Verdict

The views on the forums are very mixed. Anecdotal evidence suggests that it may be especially useful for children who are bilingual. Have a look at www.learning-solutions.co.uk/listeningprogram.php.

Cogmed

Theory

Cogmed Working Memory Training, developed in Sweden and published in the UK by Pearson, is a computerised training programme to improve working memory. There are different versions for different age groups but basically children work through a module five days a week for five weeks.

Evidence

Research suggests that poor working memory is a factor in many common conditions including dyslexia, dyspraxia, ADHD and autistic spectrum disorders. See www.cogmed.com/research for a detailed overview. One study from the University of York showed that Cogmed led to improvements in working memory, reading comprehension, attention and mathematical skills.

Drawbacks

Cogmed is a schools-based solution. Unlike other memory boosting programmes, this one involves staff being trained by a Cogmed coach. Your child's school may not be willing to go down this route.

Verdict

While programmes such as this do produce improvements in working memory, there is not a clear body of evidence that this will impact on academic performance. Children may retain and process information better but may still not produce better written work.

Fish oils

Theory

Fish oil supplements may improve the way the brain functions and help people with dyslexia, dyspraxia or ADHD.

Evidence

In 2002 there was a trial of children who had both ADHD and dyslexia who were given fish oil supplements. The trial only reported data on ADHD symptoms, which improved in the treated group. Unfortunately no results were reported for dyslexia symptoms.

Drawbacks

Some people have problems digesting oily fish. Cod liver oil tastes awful. Many supplements come with extra vitamins that can be dangerous if taken in excess, so please be careful of this.

Verdict

It's cheap and readily available. It might help improve attention, which could have a knock-on effect on reading.

> ❝ We all started taking it as my oldest son was convinced it helped brain development (brain memory and performance). I'm not sure if it helped but he certainly is functioning cognitively at a much higher level than two educational psychologist reports predicted. ❞
> Clare

The Dore programme

This is also nicknamed the 'wobbly board treatment', although it includes eye-tracking exercises as well as balancing routines.

Theory

A detailed programme of physical exercises works on the cerebellum. This is the part of the brain which lets us do things automatically. If the brain diverts power to balance, coordination and other physical skills, children can't use all their processing power for learning. Children are assessed for balance and for eye tracking and have to do daily exercises tailored to their particular needs for up to 18 months.

Evidence

There are testimonials on the Dore website along with celebrity endorsements. Kenny Logan, the ex-rugby international, has featured in newspaper articles claiming he learned to read at the age of 34 with the help of the Dore programme. Many argued that the research evidence was not independent and Ofcom found Dore's TV advertisement to be in breach of its rules on evidence, 'assessment of medical claims' and 'impressions of professional advice and support'.

Drawbacks

The programme can take up to 18 months, although most complete it in a year, so it is a big time commitment. At the time of writing, the cost is £1,925 if paid in advance, or £2,035 if paid in instalments. This covers the cost of the initial assessment too.

Verdict

It is expensive and controversial but might be worth looking into. You can read more at www.dore.co.uk.

Ben and Sarah's experience of the Dore programme

Ben had his assessment for the Dore programme in the November when he was seven. They found that his eyes were not coordinated and he was losing his place in the text if he looked up. We went away with several weeks' worth of exercises. They had to be done twice a day. The sessions had to be at least four hours apart and had to finish at least an hour before bedtime as they stimulate the brain. Ben did the exercises twice a day, seven days a week for 11 months. Sometimes he would find them very hard and frustrating but when the same exercise came round again he could see a real difference.

Once I went to collect him from a friend's house and they asked if he could stay for a sleepover. I said yes but that we had to go home first to do Ben's exercises. The mother said: 'Give the lad a break.' It was four miles away, half an hour of driving plus the petrol, but his progress was so staggering that we were all committed to it.

In just over six months his spelling age improved from five years 10 months to six years eight months and he moved up from being two years behind to being classed as average in reading, writing and comprehension. This all happened in just a few months and his confidence rocketed.

Ben is now in secondary in Year 7 and has coped really well so far. The primary school aimed to get the pupils all to level 4 and we never thought Ben would do it, but he got 4 for English, 4 for reading, and level 5 for writing, maths and science. The only problem area was Welsh, where he got a level 2. He is doing well now and does not have any extra support. He is a happy and confident child. It is like a miracle to see the progress he has made.

Chiropractic treatment

Theory

Manipulating the pelvis, spine and skull can improve the function of the spine and strongly stimulate nerve pathways to the cerebellum and other parts of the brain.

Evidence

A pilot study in Switzerland showed promising results.

Drawbacks

It can be uncomfortable. You will have to pay for a course of several sessions of treatment.

Verdict

It might be worth finding a local chiropractor who has a good reputation and seeing what they think. This might work better for children with dyspraxia.

> 66 *Rupert has had a couple of chiropractor treatments (using the McTimoney method), but more for the fact he is very tall and grows really quickly.* 99
> *Emma*

Special lenses and coloured overlays

Theory

It is estimated that about 20% of the population suffer from some form of visual stress and are unlikely to become fluent readers unless there is some kind of intervention. This might take the form of coloured overlays or tinted glasses, using a special lamp or changing the onscreen colours for reading on a computer.

Evidence

In the 1990s, Professor Arnold Wilkins carried out a series of trials to see whether colour could reduce the text distortion experienced by some readers. His research showed that coloured overlays could reduce the symptoms of visual stress and increase reading fluency in about 20% of schoolchildren, and that for five per cent of children the overlays meant that their reading speed increased by more than 25%.

Drawbacks

The cost of an initial assessment at the time of writing is £175; unfortunately it is not covered either by the NHS or by private medical insurance.

Verdict

This is well worth a look, especially if your child is rubbing his eyes or complains that the print moves around on the page or fades.

Signs of visual stress

Things to look out for that would indicate a link to vision include your child:

- rubbing his eyes
- having to use a finger to keep his place when reading
- being unable to maintain a fixed point when reading
- moving his head when reading
- saying that the print appears to get larger or smaller
- being unable to identify similarities or differences between objects
- saying that the glare from the page obscures the text
- having poor recall of information
- having poor concentration
- being unable to judge distance and speed
- having a headache and eye strain following close work
- blinking excessively.

Ask an expert

Keith Murphy is a behavioural optometrist in Warwickshire and over 200 children per year are referred to his practice.

What does the assessment involve?

We do a battery of tests looking at tracking and focusing skills, visual perception and sequential memory among other things. It's not just about vision; it is about how vision integrates with fine and gross motor skills. It is also about how the visual and auditory channels work together.

The formal assessment is expensive so we always arrange to do a routine eye check which is covered by the NHS for children under 19 in full-time education. This is then followed up by an in-depth questionnaire for the family to fill in. This means that by the time we assess a child who has dyspraxia, dyslexia or a related condition that might affect how he perceives things, we have probably ruled out the children we cannot help.

What can you do?

We can prescribe spectacles that can change spatial relationships and help with eye movements and coordination. These might have yoked prisms or be bifocals. The lenses are not like the ones you might typically find in a child's prescription because they are not about correcting sight but about changing how the visual system functions.

A second route is to use a range of vision therapy exercises to work on deficiencies and areas of weakness. These will work on gross motor coordination and retained primitive reflexes, as well as more direct visual skills. This is because visual skills develop out of gross motor development. It is now thought that children who have passed too quickly through the crawling stage can have issues with developing an awareness of space, distance and size, an awareness other children have.

Parents Active for Vision Education (P.A.V.E.) has produced DVDs to help parents encourage children's vision to develop through play. Once again, there seems to be a strong genetic component.

What about coloured filters? Do you use those?

We do use tints and filters but they would not be a first choice because they are a bit like a crutch; they enable the individual to function much better, but the underlying condition is not treated. I prefer using lenses as they have a therapeutic effect and help the individual to develop better visual skills. Having said that, there are occasions when tints and overlays are perfect, especially if you need a quick result.

How do the overlays work?

It is a spasm effect in the focusing system that makes print 'dance'. The colour in the overlays helps the focusing system to be stimulated better, and therefore controlled better, so the print keeps still.

Ben and Sarah's experience of overlays and lenses

Coloured overlays and special lenses made a difference to Ben and helped to jumpstart his reading.

Ben stalled in his reading and was taken off the reading programme. We were recommended to go and see an ophthalmic optician in Caernarvon who was a specialist in tinted glasses. I remember saying to Ben: 'Now, don't get your hopes up because this might not work!' When we got there, the optician said: 'I know you have a problem with reading but just look at these two pages and tell me which is better.' He put a tinted overlay over one and Ben said: 'That one! It's not moving.' You could have knocked me down with a feather. As someone who has worked in special needs I should be more aware that we never know how other people perceive things. They found that black text on white paper was very difficult for him to read and in addition he was getting double vision when he focused on things.

He arranged for Ben to have some tinted glasses and referred him to hospital for some eye exercises and gave him an overlay to take with him. All the way back to the car Ben was looking at street signs through the overlay and laughing. He took it into school and started to use it. He was really proud of it and his friends kept wanting to have a go too. His teacher wrote in his communication book: 'This is incredible! I have put Ben back on the reading programme and he is making really good progress.' So at the age of six, he had tinted glasses and within two weeks we could see an improvement in his coordination and he was beginning to recognise letters and numbers.

Questions to ask of a new treatment

- How does it work?
- Is there any evidence?
- Do I feel convinced by the evidence?

- When and where will the treatment take place? Will it involve a lot of travel?
- How much does it cost? This total cost might include enrolment and registration fees, many assessments, course fees, the cost of course materials and your travel costs.
- Can costs be refunded if the approach is not effective?
- Are practitioners qualified?
- How was it developed?
- How long has it been in existence?
- How many people have been treated and what was the outcome?
- How long is the course of treatment?

And remember ... be sceptical about any approach that claims to 'cure' dyslexia or dyspraxia. There are many 'quick fix' offers on the market that should be treated with caution.

13
Leaving home

Children grow up and leave home. At least that's the theory! We all wonder how our children will cope and whether the problems they have had as youngsters will affect their later life. Well, there is some good news here. While dyslexia and dyspraxia are lifelong conditions, they affect the lives of adults significantly less than those of children. There are a number of reasons for this. First of all, people learn strategies to minimise the effects of dyslexia and dyspraxia; and secondly, adults have more control over their lives.

Strategies

- **Memory:** While many have a good long-term memory and can recall information from years ago with great accuracy, short-term memory may not be so effective so it is better to do things as soon as possible after the event before memory fades.
- **Talking:** Many dyslexics and dyspraxics are much better at talking than reading and writing and may find this is a better way to do business.
- **Technology:** Some will benefit from using a voice recorder to record important events and play them back afterwards and using spell checkers and email rather than putting poor handwriting on show.
- **Utilising creative abilities:** This is not just about having a skill such as music or painting. Many people with specific learning

difficulties are so attuned to finding 'work rounds' for their own day-to-day problems that they are creative thinkers; this skill can be very much in demand.

- **Being a people person:** This probably goes with being able to 'talk the talk'. If you can make a good first impression and people like having you around, you can overcome many obstacles.

Taking control

Adults have more choices than children. For a start they can choose what to study. Jake has been to a university open day and is hoping to go to Birmingham University to study physics. Chloe is hoping to go onto higher education for a theatre course but wants a practical course rather than one in teaching or arts administration. They can choose whether to stay in education or look for a job. A lot of the time they can choose what to wear; if they decide not to wear a tie or shoes with laces, mornings become a whole lot easier. They may be able to choose their hours of work, perhaps avoiding the stresses of the rush hour, and may have some measure of control over the order in which they do things. That all depends on the job they have or the demands of an academic course. Certainly, they no longer have to play sport if they don't want to, and once they leave home they can decide on what they eat and when. With this increasing freedom come certain responsibilities: meeting deadlines, managing their time and money and being organised enough to buy food before they want to eat. However, many young people with dyspraxia and dyslexia develop their own way of doing things and relish the fact that they make decisions which suit them instead of dancing to another's tune.

Developing life skills

During the summer of 2009 the Dyspraxia Foundation ran consultative workshops for 36 young people with dyspraxia aged 12 to 25 to explore some of the issues surrounding growing up.[33] Many of the participants did not feel confident about going out by themselves. They worried about finding their way around and managing their finances. They thought they might leave money in cash machines and would spend all their money as soon as they had it. It seems that parents and schools put a lot of emphasis on support for education but do not focus enough on basic life skills such as finding their way to places, social life, road safety, going out with friends and forming adult relationships. Some of the parents featured in this book describe their children as being 'intense'. It seems as if some of them have to use so much of their energy to overcome hurdles – real or perceived – that they do not relax and enjoy themselves as much as other young people.

What can parents do?

Listen and talk – in that order. You may have got into the habit of making decisions on behalf of your child with dyspraxia or dyslexia. As they approach adulthood you need to change tactics and spend more time saying: 'What do you think?' Be sparing with your advice because you have your own way of doing things which may not be the best way for someone with specific learning difficulties. Remember the learned helplessness we talked about in Chapter 11? If we want to empower our children to find their own solutions, we need to start handing over more control to them.

- Talk about finance – make sure they have a bank account and can read a bank statement.
- Make them take control of their spending on a mobile phone.
- Encourage them to budget and do not be too ready to bail them out.
- Encourage them to develop their social life and make new friends.
- Let them make decisions about when to have a bath and what to wear.
- Be ready to listen – even at inconvenient times.

When children are small they need lots of attention. As they grow up they need less, but for most children with dyspraxia and dyslexia, when they need attention they need it from the one person they can rely on. Yes, that's you!

Will they disclose?

This is a bone of contention in some families. When a child is at school, parents and teachers will have made decisions about having a child assessed, giving him a label and ensuring that appropriate support is in place. The child does have a voice but perhaps not a very loud voice. Once the child is an adult it is up to him if he wants people to know that he has dyspraxia or dyslexia or a related condition. Chloe hopes to leave her dyslexia behind at the school gates and reinvent herself in a college of further education.

> 66 I don't want to disclose my dyslexia. I am fed up with people saying: 'Ooh dyslexia. That means you can't spell, right?' As if it was that simple! In fact my spelling is quite good. They just don't get it and I am fed up with explaining it so I would rather just get my head down and find things I am good at and build my life round that. I am going to further education college to do performing arts and I don't want school or my mum and dad to tell them I have dyslexia. I just want to be me. 99
> *Chloe*

Her parents, Linda and Will, worry about this. They worry that she will not get the help and support she needs and that her academic grades will suffer but they appreciate that this is a decision she will have to make for herself.

Some people feel that they are going to be under extra scrutiny because of their condition and will not cope well with the pressure. They worry that they may become the scapegoat and be blamed if things go wrong, and they feel that their problems are personal and no one else's business.

An employer or education provider cannot lawfully refuse someone a job or a place on a course just because he is disabled or because they do not want to make a reasonable adjustment. However, some young people feel that they may be held back in their career if their condition could have health and safety implications, for example getting drug doses right in nursing or getting the correct left-to-right orientation of a patient in radiography. On the other hand, others feel that the earlier they tell people about their needs, the easier it will be for adjustments and safeguards to be put in place in time for them to start their course or job.

The law and people with disabilities: the Equality Act 2010

- This replaced the Disability Discrimination Act 1995 (DDA). The Equality Act states that someone is disabled if 'they have a mental or physical impairment which has a substantial and long-term adverse effect on their ability to carry out normal day-to-day activities'.
- The Act covers employment, occupation, provision of goods and services (such as shopping, banking and public services), travel and transport, education, premises (buying and renting houses or flats), private clubs and public authorities.
- For example, if a woman with dyslexia is refused a job because the employer believes that people with dyslexia cannot write reports, this is unlawful under the Equality Act because it is direct discrimination.
- The Equality Act includes the duty to make reasonable adjustments if a disabled person faces problems which are 'more than minor or trivial'. This might include providing an aid or service. If the reasonable adjustment includes providing information, then it explicitly includes providing information in an accessible format, such as large print or electronically, perhaps in a Microsoft Word document or email.

- Providers of services and education providers have to plan ahead and anticipate how to meet the duty. They should not wait for you to try to use their service and then try to make the adjustment.

Benefits available to adults

Disability Living Allowance (DLA)

This was a benefit that provided for people who had personal care needs, with a second element for those with mobility problems who could not walk very far. Most people with dyspraxia who received it were given the care element at the lower rate. It is being changed to the Personal Independence Payment. There will still be two components: a daily living component and a mobility component, each with a standard and enhanced rate. The payment will still be a non-means-tested, non-taxable cash benefit that people can spend as they choose; however, it will be subject to regular reviews.

According to Maria Miller MP, Parliamentary Under-Secretary of State and Minister for Disabled People: '3.2 million people receive DLA, an increase of around 30% in the past eight years. Although we are able to reassess the level of award of any customer at any time, there is not currently any systematic way of ensuring that awards remain correct. This leaves disabled people more vulnerable to incorrect claims.' (The Government's response to the consultation on DLA reform, April 2011.)

It appears that the Personal Independence Payment will have even more stringent requirements than the DLA and that those few people with dyspraxia in receipt of this benefit may soon be disqualified.

Employment and Support Allowance

This offers access to a specially trained personal adviser and a wide range of further services, including employment, training and 'condition management' support for people to help them cope with a disability at work. It may involve a medical assessment called the Work Capability Assessment that assesses what people can do and identifies the support that they might need. Comments on the forums suggest that the advisers are not necessarily clued up about dyspraxia.

Helen's story

Helen has had a chequered time but has made positive strides to take control of her life and be independent. She has lots of stories and practical ideas for making life easier so she provides us a glimpse of what may lie ahead for your children in future years and gives you a chance to reflect on your own parenting.

Helen was found to have dyslexia when she was six. Her mother was determined to do the best for her and tried everything she could think of to help her to overcome what she saw as 'Helen's problem'. She checked her homework every night, employed a private tutor twice a week and made sure she went to a specialist centre every Saturday morning.

Helen says: 'Then she got a bee in her bonnet about E numbers. She had read somewhere that they had a bad effect on concentration. So I had a year of no squash, no crisps, no sweets, and no birthday cake. I really resented other children, who didn't have all this fuss. Even the hamster had more fun than I did!'

Helen left home at the age of 17 and had her daughter by the time she was 18.

'I would not recommend this to others because it was very hard going but I did discover a lot about myself and found that really I was quite competent. I had some problems once I left home but I also learned that I could sort them out for myself. I got a part-time job in a pets' supplies store and loved it from the beginning. Suddenly I was the one who knew about fish and how to care for them. Also I was the one they called for to charm difficult customers. It must have been all that practice I had dealing with my mum!'

Now Helen works for a cosmetics company and travels all around the country.

Driving

Many people with dyspraxia and dyslexia have some form of visual perception problems and they may find it hard to judge speed and distance. Working out if a car will fit into a space can be harder for them than for others. These days everyone has to do the theory test too, but there are books, videos and CD-ROMs which mean that people can practise at home until they are confident. You can apply for extra time for the test; you can request to have up to double the time for the multiple-choice part. If you do need more than the normal time, you must send proof of your reading difficulty to the theory test booking customer services. If you have dyslexia or other reading difficulties, you can ask for an English or Welsh voiceover.

Helen found her own solutions to some of these problems.

> 66 Learning to drive was a challenge. I spent an absolute fortune learning to drive, or rather trying to. Nothing fell into place for ages and I had a real problem with which way to turn the wheel when I was reversing. I know other people have these problems but I just could not make sense of what I was seeing in the rear view mirror. I could not work out if cars were coming or going. Two things helped: I had a friend who insured me on his car, which was an automatic, so I sorted out a lot of stuff in my head without having to worry about the gears as well. The other thing was that I finally cracked left and right. My friend spent ages saying 'Turn your way, turn my way' but that wasn't going to work in a driving test so I taped coloured arrows to the dashboard. I still remember them as 'Mellow Yellow Left' and 'Red is Right'. 99
> Helen

Hints and tips

- Some driving schools start with simulated lessons so a learner develops skills before going out on the road.

- Find a driving school where instructors have experience of dyspraxia and dyslexia.
- Perhaps, like Helen, start learning to drive on an automatic to cut down on the number of skills to be mastered.
- If your child loses belongings regularly, make sure you keep a spare set of car keys.

Organisational skills

If your child seems to be 'permanently in a fog', as one mother put it, then encourage him to use a small notepad or organiser or put notes on his mobile phone. Try to get him to plan ahead, and if things go wrong, instead of apportioning blame, get him to reflect on how he can avoid the same mistakes in the future. Once again, while it is tempting to tell your child how to do things, in the long run it is not a helpful strategy. After all, you are not making those mistakes so your solution may not be the best one.

> 66 Travel can be a problem because I am not always as organised as I should be but I have a system now. I have a checklist of what I should have in my case, otherwise there is a danger that I will turn up with no comb or no underwear. I also usually have a bag – contact lens stuff, toothpaste, deodorant – which just stays in the case, but there has been more than one occasion when I have unpacked only to remember I needed fresh supplies. It's always 11.30 at night in a hotel on some industrial estate miles from shops when that happens. I have to keep track of dates, times of appointments, addresses, train times, flight numbers. I put the essential information all together in one document in large print. 99
> Helen

Time and money

Being in the right place at the right time is an art. Our families suggested several strategies. Use a timer, set alarms on a mobile, check and print out timetables and always factor in extra time for travel. Budgeting is a key concern too. Hopefully, before they reach the age of 18 you will already have helped your child learn how to budget and made him aware of the perils of overdrafts, store cards and credit cards. While all these things can be useful, spending can spiral out of control. A really useful resource for young people is TheSite.Org (www.thesite.org). Helen believes that it is important to check her balance regularly.

> 66 *Outside work I have the same problems as other people: managing my time and money. I don't always manage my money well but I am getting better. I round everything up so hopefully there is a little extra in the kitty or, if I've calculated it wrong, at least I'm not as overdrawn as I could have been. Part of the problem is that I forget numbers very easily. I would get money out of a cash point and realise that there was not much left in but then I would forget what the balance was. So I started to get a receipt each time as a record but then I would lose the receipt. I have cracked that with online banking. I have a smartphone and can check it any time I want. I think it helps me to be more organised.* 99
> *Helen*

She also has some hints and tips for keeping track of pin numbers and passwords.

> 66 *You have to be so careful not to carry them round or leave them where they can be found so you need to use your memory. I have lots of frustrations. I try a password and it is rejected and I don't know whether the problem is my spelling or if I've got the wrong word altogether. Now I try to have just three passwords and one of them is the first line of my favourite song. I sing it in my head and the first letter of each word makes up my password. It works for me.* 99
> *Helen*

Technology is a lifeline

People used to think that dyslexics and dyspraxics had to master skills and then move on to technology: perfect their handwriting and then use a keyboard; work hard on their spelling and then use a spell checker. But technology has revolutionised the way people work. It is so easy to save, store and edit text so you can reuse it instead of always starting from scratch with each piece of writing. Templates can help with the layout and structure of CVs and letters. The internet gives people instant access to information, and with a text-to-speech system as discussed in Chapter 9, they can listen to text or save it as a file to an MP3 player. There is no doubt that technology has changed the way we work and study. It can be a real safety net for young people as they become more independent. With a mobile, they can phone if they need information or advice. Sometimes this is a mixed blessing for parents. You want them to check in with home but not necessarily when you are sound asleep. Helen finds that technology has made her life much simpler.

> 66 *These days I use a satnav. It has taken so much stress out of driving to new places. I can just relax and listen to the directions. I know satnavs are not perfect but they always get me to my destination one way or another.*
>
> *My phone is my lifeline. I have everything on there. I do now have a separate printed list with all my phone numbers in case I lose the phone and it is also on the computer in case I lose the list. That's the difference between me and my friends. They always seem surprised if they lose their phone but it happens to me so often that I have a strategy and am prepared for it. See? Dyslexia does have advantages!* 99
> *Helen*

Remember

- Children with dyslexia and dyspraxia will grow up to lead independent lives.
- As they approach adulthood they have more opportunities to make their own decisions and this can minimise some of the problems they have faced as children.
- Listen carefully and do not rush to offer advice. You are not the one with dyspraxia or dyslexia.
- Help your child to develop skills and strategies for coping.
- It is a personal decision whether or not to disclose conditions to employers or university.
- Learning to drive can be more difficult for young people with dyslexia and dyspraxia than for others.
- Travel plans may test the organisational skills of those with specific learning difficulties.
- Technology – computers, the internet, smartphones, satnav, online banking – can be useful allies.

Glossary

Aphasia: A disorder of language. Your ability to understand and express words is affected. Aphasia can affect the understanding of speech, reading, speaking, writing, gesture and signing.

Apraxia: The inability to control fine and gross motor movement and gestures. The disorder can also affect communication skills. Apraxia can range from mild to severe. People with apraxia often cannot perform controlled, purposeful movement, despite having the physical strength and intellectual thought and desire to do so. It is more severe than dyspraxia.

Attention deficit disorder (ADD): Characterised by an inability to concentrate. Children may be prone to daydreaming and avoidance strategies. They can appear to be slow and anxious.

Attention deficit hyperactivity disorder (ADHD): Affects three to five per cent of all children. Two to three times more boys than girls are affected. It has been described as 'living in a kaleidoscope, where sounds, images and thoughts are constantly shifting'. A child will feel easily bored and distracted by unimportant sounds and sights. They will be unable to sit still and will dash around incessantly.

Auditory processing: How you internalise sound. Problems may mean information is not decoded or remembered correctly. Children may appear confused and may not be able to block out competing background noises. Sequencing difficulties may result in a language disorder.

Auditory sequential memory: The ability to hear a sequence, hold it in the mind and act on it, e.g. looking up a phone number and dialling it.

Bilateral integration: The ability to move both sides of the body in opposing ways, e.g. the crawl in swimming.

Cognitive functioning: Mental processes such as thinking, understanding and remembering.

Cognitive style: The usual way you approach learning or problem solving – your 'learning style'.

Compensatory strategies: Alternative, faster or harder methods that you use to get round your weaknesses.

Decoding words: Recognising the individual letters in a word, what sounds in a word (phonemes) they represent, and blending them together to sound out and identify the words.

Dyscalculia: A specific difficulty with maths and numbers.

Dysgraphia: A specific difficulty with writing, including spelling, sentence structure and handwriting.

Dysphasia: A specific difficulty with speech and language patterns.

Expressive language difficulty: A difficulty in putting thought into words, symbols or signs. Your ability to speak, write or gesture.

Fine motor skills: 'Nimble fingers' or the ability to use your fingers for small, neat movements, e.g. handwriting or threading a needle.

Gross motor skills: The ability to carry out 'big' movements, e.g. kicking, throwing and crawling.

Hemispheres: The two parts of the brain (left and right). Each hemisphere is said to specialise in different thought processes.

Hereditary: A characteristic that is passed from one generation of a family to another. Dyslexia and dyspraxia often run in families.

Hypersensitivity: An excessive reaction to texture. Some children with dyspraxia cannot bear to touch finger paints, clay, etc.

Hyposensitivity: The lack of reaction to touch. You may find handling objects or materials difficult.

Individual educational plan (IEP): Outlines what help a child should receive and targets to work towards.

Kinaesthetic learning: Learning through physical activity rather than just sitting still.

Meares-Irlen Syndrome: A problem with eyes that causes physical discomfort when reading. It can cause slow reading, frustration, tiredness, headaches and mistakes. Lines may appear to jump, move or distort. Problems get worse when reading small print on white or shiny paper. The use of special coloured glasses or a transparent plastic overlay over text can bring relief. Other terms similar in meaning include: Scotopic Sensitivity Syndrome; Colour Sensitivity; Irlen Syndrome.

Midline crossing: The ability to pass the hand across the body, e.g. when handwriting or playing tennis.

Neurological: Relating to the functioning and structure of the brain and nervous system.

Obsessive compulsive disorder (OCD): Repetitive behaviours caused by anxiety, apprehension, fear or worry.

Occupational therapy: Training people to perform the tasks of daily living at home, at work or in the classroom.

Percentile rank: A system of grading you in comparison to a similar group of 100 people. For example, if 100 students of a similar age took a spelling test and you scored in the 30th percentile, that would mean that on average 69% of students would score better than you, and 29% would score less well.

Phonemes: The smallest units of speech that distinguish one spoken sound from another and are written as single letters or groups of letters that make one sound, e.g. b, st and ch.

Phonetics: The study of the sounds of spoken words and letters.

Phonics: A method used to teach students to pronounce and read words by learning the phonetic sounds of letters, letter groups and syllables. It is based on learning phonemes.

Phonological awareness: Knowledge of how letters of the alphabet represent speech sounds. The ability to identify numbers of syllables, to rhyme, to blend and to segment words into syllables and sound.

Portage: Home-based educational support for pre-school children with special educational needs.

Pragmatic disorder: Using language inappropriately in a particular situation.

Proprioception: Body awareness or awareness of where your body parts are in relation to the space around you and how they move.

Public equality duty (PED): Came into force in April 2011 and requires public authorities such as local authorities, the NHS and schools to eliminate discrimination, harassment and victimisation, to promote equality of opportunity, and to foster good relations. The Equality Act says that in order to do this public authorities may need to treat disabled people more favourably.

Reading age: Represents the average level of reading skills expected for a child of that age.

Receptive language difficulty: A difficulty affecting your ability to understand and process language.

School Action: When a teacher provides help that is extra to or different from that provided as part of the school's usual differentiated curriculum.

School Action Plus: When a school involves outside specialists, e.g. specialist teachers, educational psychologists, speech and language therapists or other health professionals.

Sensory integration: The ability to take in information from your senses and make use of it.

Sequencing skills: The ability to arrange letters, words, numbers, ideas or tasks in a formal or logical structure. This is often seen as an area of weakness for people with dyslexia.

Short-term memory: The ability to hold information for a matter of seconds or minutes, e.g. holding a spelling in your head while you find a definition in a dictionary.

Spatial awareness: The ability to judge distance and orientation.

Special Educational Needs and Disability Tribunal (SENDIST): The First-tier Tribunal for Special Educational Needs and Disability was set up by the Education Act 1993. It considers parents' appeals against the decisions of local authorities about children's special educational needs if parents cannot reach agreement with the local authority. It is totally independent.

Special educational needs coordinator (SENCO): The teacher with responsibility for coordinating special help for children with special educational needs at their school.

Special school: A school that is just for pupils with statements of special educational needs.

Specific learning difficulty: A difficulty with a particular aspect of learning rather than with all learning tasks. Dyslexia is seen as a specific learning difficulty.

Speech and language therapy (SALT): Assessing and treating speech, language and communication problems to help children understand what is said to them and to enable them to communicate to the best of their ability.

Speed of information processing: Refers to how long it takes you to make sense of and use visual or auditory information.

Spelling age: See 'Reading Age' above.

Standardised: When a test score is 'standardised', that means that an average score has been worked out for people of a particular age.

Statement of special educational needs: A document that sets out children's needs and all the extra help they should receive.

Symmetrical integration: The ability to move both sides of the body simultaneously, e.g. to jump or clap hands.

Synapses: The neural pathways or connections in the brain that fire up during the early years. These are pruned in late childhood in most children. One theory is that they are not pruned as efficiently in children with dyspraxia and dyslexia. As a result they have more potential pathways in the brain, which can make for slower processing and less traditional patterns of thought.

Tactile perception: How things feel. Children with dyspraxia may experience hypersensitivity, so they will not touch finger paints, clay, etc. They may overreact to even the slightest touch. Hyposensitivity means that they do not respond to touch and may find handling objects and materials difficult.

Tracking problems: The inability to read a line of print from left to right. Some learners see the whole and therefore read from all directions at once. They need to use a reading ruler or their finger to keep their eyes focused on the line.

Verbal dyspraxia: A coordination difficulty. The brain transmits the wrong messages about when and how the muscles of the throat and mouth should move to make voice and speech. Speech may sound muddled because the wrong sounds are produced in the wrong places.

Visual perception: Judgement of distance, depth, height, etc. Problems may show up as poor gross motor skills (e.g. throwing and catching a ball) or poor fine motor skills (e.g. inability to control a pencil).

Word recognition: The ability to accurately recognise and understand a word that you read.

Further reading and useful contacts

Organisations for dyslexia

British Dyslexia Association: www.bdadyslexia.org.uk; 0845 251 9002
Dyslexia Action: www.dyslexiaaction.org.uk; 01784 222300
Dyslexia SpLD Trust: www.thedyslexia-spldtrust.org.uk; 01344 381564. A group of voluntary and community organisations.
dyslexic.com: www.dyslexic.com; 01223 420209. Technology for dyslexia.
Helen Arkell Dyslexia Centre: www.arkellcentre.org.uk; 01252 792 400. Specialist dyslexia organisation which offers courses.
Send a lot of flowers? Visit www.charityflowers.co.uk/store and they will donate 15% of the price to Dyslexia Action, at no extra cost to you.

Organisations for dyspraxia

Dyspraxia Foundation: www.dyspraxiafoundation.org.uk; 01462 454 986.
Dyscovery Centre: http://dyscovery.newport.ac.uk; 01633 432330. Good advice and resources for dyspraxia.
Matts Hideout: www.matts-hideout.co.uk. A blog going back several years and written by Matt, who has dyspraxia.
SpeechDisorder: www.speechdisorder.co.uk. This site has a section on dyspraxia.

More general organisations

AbilityNet: www.abilitynet.org.uk; 0870 240 4455. Assistive technology for a range of issues, including dyspraxia and dyslexia.

British Association of Behavioural Optometrists: www.babo.co.uk;
01256 862547.
College of Occupational Therapists: www.cot.org.uk/Homepage;
020 7357 6480.
Education Otherwise: www.education-otherwise.net; 0845 478
6345. Home schooling website.
Irlen: www.irlenuk.com; regional centres each have their
own phone number – check the website for local numbers.
Information on visual stress assessment, coloured overlays and
lenses.
National Parent Partnership Network: www.parentpartnership.
org.uk; 020 7843 6058.
Right to Read campaign: www.rnib.org.uk/righttoread. An
alliance of 19 charities campaigning for people with print
impairments, including dyslexia and dyspraxia, to have access to
the same book, at the same time and the same price as everyone
else. This could include e-books and downloadable audio books.
Springboard for Children: www.springboard.org.uk; 020 7921
4550. Literacy organisation with an inner-city focus.
Xtraordinary People: www.xtraordinarypeople.com. Famous
people with dyspraxia and dyslexia.

Forums

Being Dyslexic: www.beingdyslexic.co.uk.
Dyslexia Parents Resource: www.dyslexia-parent.com.
Dyspraxic Teens: www.dyspraxicteens.org.uk.
mumsnet: www.mumsnet.com.

Dyslexia fiction for young people

Theresa Breslin *Whispers in the Graveyard*
A fantasy thriller about a dyslexic boy called Solomon who likes
to hide in the local graveyard. When workmen start to disturb the
graves an ancient and evil power is released.
Rob Childs *Moving the Goalposts*

A comic book about Sam the star goalkeeper who has dyslexia.
Anne Fine *How to Write Really Badly*
Know-it-all Chester is scornful of Joe's learning difficulties.
However, in the end he is an unexpected source of support.
Julia Jarman *Ghost Writer*
Frankie Ruggles DBNS (Dyslexic But Not Stupid) becomes
involved in trying to help a boy from a century ago who may have
been dyslexic too.
Tom Palmer *Reading the Game*
Ben is a brilliant footballer but he can't read. With team sheets
and game reports to follow, keeping his secret is becoming
harder and harder. Eventually his actions threaten to put his place
in the team in jeopardy.
Rick Riordan *Percy Jackson and the Battle of the Labyrinth*
This is the fourth book in the series about Percy Jackson, a
12-year-old boy who happens to be both dyslexic and the son of
a Greek god! This will appeal to fans of Harry Potter and Artemis
Fowl.
Jacqueline Wilson *The Illustrated Mum*
Dyslexic Dolphin and her sister Star are by turns delighted and
disturbed by their depressive mum, who has a new tattoo for
every celebration in their lives.

Good books for parents

Atter, Elizabeth and Drew, Sharon, *Can't Play Won't Play: Simply
Sizzling Ideas to Get the Ball Rolling for Children with Dyspraxia*
(Jessica Kingsley, 2008).
Biggs, Victoria, *Caged in Chaos: A Dyspraxic Guide to Breaking
Free* (Jessica Kingsley, 2005).
Christmas, Jill, *Hands on Dyspraxia: Supporting Children and
Young People with Sensory and Motor Learning Challenges*
(Speechmark Publishing, 2009).
Kirby, Amanda, *Dyspraxia: Developmental Co-ordination
Disorder* (Souvenir Press, 1999).
Kirby, Amanda and Drew, Sharon, *Guide to Dyspraxia and
Developmental Coordination Disorders* (David Fulton Books,
2003).

Likierman, Helen and Muter, Valerie, *Prepare Your Child for School: How to Make Sure Your Child Gets Off to a Flying Start* (Vermilion, 2006).

Handwriting books

Addy, Lois, *Speed Up!: A Kinaesthetic Programme to Develop Fluent Handwriting* (LDA, 2004).
Sassoon, Rosemary, *Handwriting: The Way to Teach It* (Sage Publications, 2003).
Taylor, Jane, *Handwriting: A Teacher's Guide – Multisensory approaches to assessing and improving handwriting skills* (David Fulton Books, 2001).
Teodorescu, Ion and Addy, Lois, *Write from the Start: The Teodorescu Perceptuo-Motor Programme – Developing the fine motor and perceptual skills for effective handwriting*, 3 volumes (LDA, 1998).

Endnotes

1. www.beingdyslexic.co.uk
2. www.dyspraxiafoundation.org.uk; www.dyslexiaaction.org.uk
3. 'The dyslexic boy failed by the system' by David Cohen, *Evening Standard*, 20 June 2011.
4. 'Dyslexic entrepreneurs: the incidence; their coping strategies and their business skills' by Julie Logan. In *Dyslexia*, vol. 15, no. 4. (2009), pp328–46.
5. 'Dear parent: why your dyslexic child struggles with reading' by Maryanne Wolf, *Guardian*, 9 May 2011.
6. www.dyspraxiafoundation.org.uk
7. www.devdis.com
8. To access the full Rose Review, go to: www.education.gov.uk/publications
9. www.dailymail.co.uk/health/article-4146/Be-kinder-baby-boys.html
10. See also www.beingdyslexic.co.uk and 'Brain Scans Show Dyslexics Read Better with Alternative Strategies' by Abigail Marshall (2003), accessed at www.dyslexia.com/science/different_pathways.htm
11. 'Dear parent: why your dyslexic child struggles with reading' by Maryanne Wolf, *Guardian*, 9 May 2011.
12. *The Buzan Study Skills Handbook: The Shortcut to Success in Your Studies with Mind Mapping, Speed Reading and Winning Memory Techniques* by Tony Buzan (BBC Active, 2006).
13. *Supporting Children with Dyslexia* by Garry Squires and Sally McKeown (Continuum International Publishing Group, 2006).
14. Dyspraxia Foundation Survey of Parents of Children with Dyspraxia, 1997: www.dyspraxiafoundation.org.uk
15. Dyspraxia Foundation Survey of Educational Provision for Pupils with Dyspraxia, June 2006: www.dyspraxiafoundation.org.uk
16. http://eduwight.iow.gov.uk/the_lea/policies_plans/images/QualityFirstTeaching.pdf
17. Jeff Hughes's website is www.box42.com
18. www.popat.co.uk
19. www.oup.co.uk/oxed/primary/sen/fuzzbuzz [username and password required]

20. 'The dyspraxia myth' by Michael Weber, *Evening Standard*, 16 July 2004.

21. The Disability Discrimination Act has been replaced by the Equality Act 2010. For details of the SEN Code of Practice, see the Department for Education website: www.education.gov.uk

22. www.crested.org.uk

23. www.amandamcleod.org

24. *ACE Spelling Dictionary* by David Moseley (LDA, 2009).

25. *The Buzan Study Skills Handbook: The Shortcut to Success in Your Studies with Mind Mapping, Speed Reading and Winning Memory Techniques* by Tony Buzan (BBC Active, 2006).

26. www.elevenplusexams.co.uk/forum/11plus/memberlist. php?mode=viewprofile&u=3994 [You need to be registered to access the posts on this forum]

27. Jane Mitchell's website is www.calsc.co.uk

28. www.youngminds.org.uk

29. www.eric.org.uk

30. www.dyspraxicteens.org.uk/forum

31. 'Daniel Radcliffe: breaking dyspraxia's spell' by Fiona Macdonald-Smith, *The Telegraph*, 15 September 2008.

32. www.thinkuknow.co.uk/parents/safeuse/

33. Findings from a national consultation with young people living with dyspraxia, 2009: www.dyspraxiafoundation.org.uk

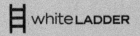
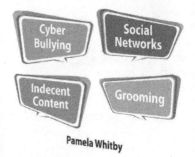